NO LONGER PROPERTY OF
SEATTLE PUBLIC LIBRARY

W9-CTR-553

# Celebrate Christmas

## WITH THAT PATCHWORK PLACE®

## 22 Festive Projects to Quilt and Sew

Martingale®
Create with Confidence

Celebrate Christmas with That Patchwork Place®:
22 Festive Projects to Quilt and Sew

© 2014 by Martingale & Company®

Martingale®
19021 120th Ave. NE, Ste. 102
Bothell, WA 98011-9511 USA
ShopMartingale.com

No part of this product may be reproduced in any form, unless otherwise stated, in which case reproduction is limited to the use of the purchaser. The written instructions, photographs, designs, projects, and patterns are intended for the personal, noncommercial use of the retail purchaser and are under federal copyright laws; they are not to be reproduced by any electronic, mechanical, or other means, including informational storage or retrieval systems, for commercial use. Permission is granted to photocopy patterns for the personal use of the retail purchaser. Attention teachers: Martingale encourages you to use this book for teaching, subject to the restrictions stated above.

The information in this book is presented in good faith, but no warranty is given nor results guaranteed. Since Martingale has no control over choice of materials or procedures, the company assumes no responsibility for the use of this information.

Printed in China

19 18 17 16 15 14    8 7 6 5 4 3 2 1

Library of Congress Cataloging-in-Publication Data is available upon request.

ISBN: 978-1-60468-388-2

## Mission Statement

Dedicated to providing quality products and service to inspire creativity.

## Credits

PRESIDENT AND CEO: Tom Wierzbicki

EDITOR IN CHIEF: Mary V. Green

DESIGN DIRECTOR: Paula Schlosser

MANAGING EDITOR: Karen Costello Soltys

ACQUISITIONS EDITOR: Karen M. Burns

TECHNICAL EDITOR: Laura Stone Roberts

COPY EDITOR: Sheila Chapman Ryan

PRODUCTION MANAGER: Regina Girard

COVER AND INTERIOR DESIGNER: Connor Chin

PHOTOGRAPHER: Brent Kane

ILLUSTRATOR: Christine Erikson

## Project Designers

Mary Burns

Jenny Wilding Cardon

Diane Chin

Leanne Clare

Claudia L'Heureux Cole

Cornelia Heitz Gauger

Mary V. Green

Karen Morrell Johnson

Tiffany Mottet

Tracy Overturf

Cathy Valentine Reitan

Adrienne Smitke

Karen Costello Soltys

# Contents

# O Christmas Tree
# Wall Hanging

Not everyone has room for a towering noble fir Christmas tree in their home. This wall hanging doubles as a fresh take on holiday decor *and* as a place to gather presents (and your family) on Christmas morning. It would also make a wonderful gift for anyone who wants a Christmas tree substitute that can be used year after year.

Designed and pieced by Adrienne Smitke; machine quilted by Lisa Sipes | Finished wall hanging: 28¼" x 44½"

## Materials

*Yardage is based on 42"-wide fabric.*

1¼ yards of gray print for background

⅝ yard of white-on-white print for tree

¼ yard of green print #1 for zigzag

¼ yard of green print #2 for zigzag

4½" x 9" piece of green print #3 for zigzag

¼ yard of red print #1 for zigzag

¼ yard of red print #2 for zigzag and binding

⅜ yard of red print #3 for zigzag and binding

3" x 6" piece of charcoal print for tree trunk

1⅝ yards of fabric for backing and hanging sleeve

34" x 50" piece of batting

## Cutting

**From the gray print, cut:**
1 strip, 5½" x 42"; crosscut into 2 strips, 5½" x 13⅜"
2 rectangles, 14½" x 36½"
1 strip, 3½" x 28¼"

**From the white-on-white print, cut:**
3 strips, 4" x 42"; crosscut into 28 squares, 4" x 4"
4 squares, 3½" x 3½"

**From the green print #1, cut:**
1 strip, 4" x 42"; crosscut into 8 squares, 4" x 4"

**From the green print #2, cut:**
1 strip, 4" x 42"; crosscut into 6 squares, 4" x 4"

**From the green print #3, cut:**
2 squares, 4" x 4"

**From the red print #1, cut:**
1 strip, 4" x 42"; crosscut into 6 squares, 4" x 4"

**From the red print #2, cut:**
1 strip, 4" x 42"; crosscut into 4 squares, 4" x 4"
1 strip, 2¼" x 42"

**From the red print #3, cut:**
3 strips, 2¼" x 42"
2 squares, 4" x 4"

**From the charcoal print, cut:**
1 rectangle, 2½" x 5½"

## Making the Half-Square-Triangle Units

1. Draw a diagonal line from corner to corner on the wrong side of a white 4" square. Layer the square on a green #1 square, right sides together, and stitch ¼" from the line on both sides. Cut the squares apart on the drawn line to make two half-square-triangle units. Press the seam allowances away from the white triangles. Trim the units to measure 3½" x 3½". Make a total of 16 half-square-triangle units.

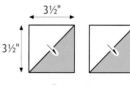

Green #1 unit.
Make 16.

2. Repeat step 1, pairing the remaining green and red 4" squares with white squares to make the number of half-square-triangle units indicated below.

Green #2 unit.
Make 12.

Green #3 unit.
Make 4.

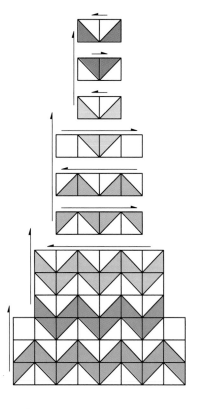

Red #1 unit.
Make 12 .

Red #2 unit.
Make 8.

Red #3 unit.
Make 4.

## Piecing the Christmas Tree Unit

1. Watching the orientation of the units, lay out the four white 3½" squares and the half-square-triangle units in 12 rows as shown below. Join the pieces into rows and press the seam allowances in opposite directions from row to row.

2. Sew the rows together, aligning the center seams. Press the seam allowances toward the top of the tree.

## Aligning Uneven Rows

When sewing together rows with different numbers of units, match up the center seams of adjoining rows and pin to secure in place. Working outward, continue to align seams and pin, using plenty of pins to keep the rows correctly aligned.

## Assembling the Wall Hanging

1. With the fabric right side up, use an erasable fabric marker to mark the bottom edge of one of the gray 14½" x 36½" rectangles, 2¼" from the bottom-left corner as shown. In the same manner, mark 2¼" from the bottom-right corner of the second gray rectangle. Using a ruler, draw a diagonal line from each of the marks to the opposite top corner of its rectangle. Cut the rectangles apart on the drawn lines to make mirror-image background pieces. Discard the cut-away triangles.

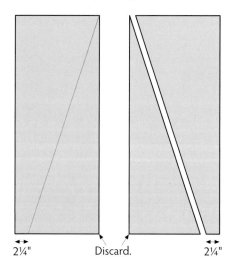

2¼"                Discard.                2¼"

2. On the wrong side of the gray background pieces, mark a dot ¼" from each raw edge at the corners along the angled edge. In the same manner, mark the right side of the pieced

Christmas tree unit at each bottom corner and ¼" to each side of the center seam, ¼" from the top of the tree.

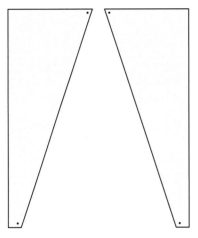

Mark ¼" from *both* corners on angled edge.

3. Lay the marked gray piece for the left side of the tree, right sides together with the Christmas tree unit, on a flat surface with the gray fabric on top. Align the marks at the bottom corners of both pieces and pin to secure in place. Align the mark at the top of the gray piece with the mark *to the right of the center seam* on the Christmas tree unit (raw edges will not align). Pin to secure in place. The seam line for these two pieces should intersect the outside corners at the ends of the rows of green #3 blocks, red #2 blocks, and red #1 blocks. For a tip on accurate alignment, see "Easy Alignment with Painter's Tape" at right.

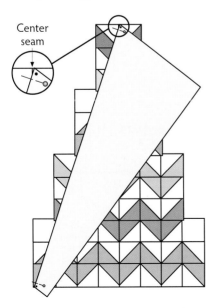

Center seam

Because the seam is long and a bit unwieldy to line up, Adrienne used painter's tape to help align the pieces correctly. Use the center seam at the top of the tree unit and the intersections of the seams (indicated below) at the end of the rows of green #3, red #2, and red #1 blocks as guides for placing the painters tape. Align the edge of the textured gray-print background piece to the inside edge of the tape, making sure to match the pins at each end. Open the unit and make sure the top and bottom edges of the background and the Christmas tree unit are aligned. By waiting to trim the Christmas tree unit until after you're sure you've sewn this seam accurately, there's always the option of ripping out the seam and realigning the pieces, if need be.

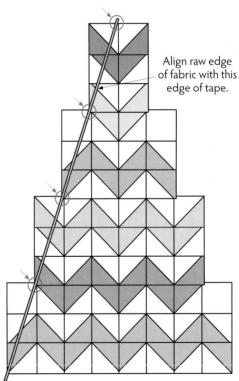

Align raw edge of fabric with this edge of tape.

Align the painter's tape on the *outside* of the marks made in step 2 on page 6 and intersect the corners of the blocks as indicated. Align the background fabric to the *inside* edge of the tape and pin in place.

4. Stitch through both layers ¼" from the raw edge of the background piece. Open the unit and make sure the top and bottom edges of the background and the Christmas tree unit are aligned before trimming the Christmas tree unit even with the background piece. Press the seam allowances toward the background piece. Repeat steps 3 and 4 with the second gray background piece.

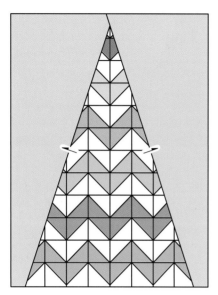

5. Sew the gray 5½" x 13⅜" strips to opposite sides of the charcoal 2½" x 5½" rectangle. Press the seam allowances toward the gray strips.

6. Sew the unit from step 5 to the bottom of the Christmas tree. Sew the gray 3½" x 28¼" strip to the top. Press the seam allowances toward the strips.

## Finishing the Wall Hanging

For help with any of the finishing steps, go to ShopMartingale.com/HowtoQuilt for free downloadable information.

1. Cut the backing fabric so it's 4" to 6" larger than the quilt top on all sides, leaving a 6"- to 8"-wide lengthwise strip of fabric for the hanging sleeve. Layer and baste the quilt top, batting, and backing.

2. Quilt as desired. What makes this simple wall hanging really pop is the beautiful machine quilting. Lisa used a combination of brick and spiral motifs for the background, inspired by a memory of setting up her family's Christmas tree in front of a brick wall in her childhood home. On the zigzag rows of the tree, she alternated a pebble motif with a beaded chain reminiscent of hand-strung popcorn garlands.

3. Use the 6"- to 8"-wide lengthwise strip of backing fabric to make a hanging sleeve; baste the sleeve top edges to the top of the wall-hanging back. Using the 2¼"-wide red #2 and #3 strips, prepare and sew the binding to the quilt, and then finish attaching the sleeve.

# Snowflakes Quilt

Combine easy blocks and quick raw-edge appliqué in this throw-sized quilt that will ward off the winter chill—and keep you cozy from first snowfall to last!

| Designed, pieced, and quilted by Jenny Wilding Cardon | Finished quilt: 54½" x 63½" Finished block: 9" x 9" |
| --- | --- |

## Materials

*Yardage is based on 42"-wide fabric. Jenny used "Aspen Frost" fabrics by Basic Grey for Moda.*

2⅞ yards of light-blue snowflake print for blocks and binding

1⅞ yards of white-on-white print for blocks and appliqués

1¼ yards of medium-turquoise print for blocks and binding

3¾ yards of fabric for backing

61" x 70" piece of batting

Washable glue stick

Quarter or other medium-sized coin

## Cutting

**From the light-blue snowflake print, cut:**
28 squares, 10" x 10"
3 squares, 9½" x 9½"
12 strips, 2" x 12½"

**From the white-on-white print, cut:**
72 squares, 5" x 5"
Reserve the remaining white print for appliqués.

**From the medium-turquoise print, cut:**
8 squares, 10" x 10"
3 squares, 9½" x 9½"
12 strips, 2" x 12½"

## Making the Pieced Blocks

1. Draw a diagonal line from corner to corner on the wrong side of each white 5" square. Place a marked square on one corner of a light-blue 10" square, right sides together and raw edges aligned. Sew on the marked line. Trim the excess corner fabric, leaving a ¼" seam allowance. Flip the corner triangle open and press the seam allowances toward the blue square. Repeat on the opposite corner of the blue square to complete one pieced square. Make 28.

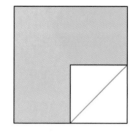
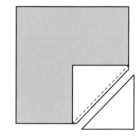

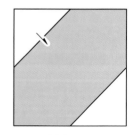

Make 28.

2. In the same manner, use 16 white squares and 8 medium-turquoise 10" squares to make 8 pieced squares.

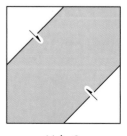

Make 8.

3. Cut the 36 pieced squares made in steps 1 and 2 in half diagonally to yield 72 pieced triangles. Sew two light-blue/white triangles together along their long edges to make one blue/white pieced block. Press the seam allowances open to reduce bulk. Repeat to make a total of 28 blue/white pieced blocks. In the same manner, use the remaining blue/white triangles and the turquoise/white triangles to make a total of eight turquoise/blue pieced blocks. Trim all 36 blocks to measure 9½" x 9½".

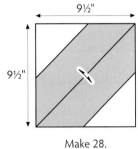

Make 28.  Make 8.

## Making the Snowflake Blocks

1. Trace the snowflake pattern (page 12) onto cardstock (a bright light or window behind the template makes this easier) and cut it out. Trace 36 snowflake shapes onto the *wrong* side of the remaining white print, leaving at least ½" of space between the shapes. Cut out the shapes just inside the drawn lines.

2. Fold a light-blue 9½" square in half vertically and horizontally to find the center point. Place a quarter over the center point, dabbing a bit of the glue stick on the coin to keep it in place.

Position six snowflake appliqués evenly spaced around the quarter, so that their tips are just touching the edge of the quarter. Dab the appliqués with a tiny bit of the glue stick to keep them in place for raw-edge machine appliqué. Remove the quarter.

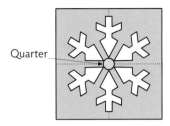

Quarter

3. Using white thread, topstitch a scant ¼" from the raw edges of the appliqués to secure them. When you reach the tip of each snowflake appliqué, stitch to the point, backstitch, and then continue around the shape as before.

4. Repeat steps 2–4 to make a total of three Snowflake blocks with light-blue backgrounds and three Snowflake blocks with turquoise backgrounds.

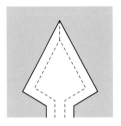

Make 3.  Make 3.

## Assembling the Quilt Top

Using the quilt photo (below) as a guide, lay out the blocks in seven rows of six blocks each. Sew the blocks into rows and press the seam allowances in opposite directions from row to row. Sew the rows together and press the seam allowances in one direction.

## Finishing the Quilt

For help with any of the finishing steps, go to ShopMartingale.com/HowtoQuilt for free downloadable information.

1. Cut the backing fabric so it's 4" to 6" larger than the quilt top on all sides. Layer the quilt top, batting, and backing; baste the layers together.

2. Hand or machine quilt as desired.

3. Alternating colors, join the light-blue and turquoise 12½"-long strips by layering the strips, right sides together, at a right angle and sewing across the diagonal as shown. Trim ¼" from

the stitching line and press the seam allowances open. Bind the quilt with the pieced binding.

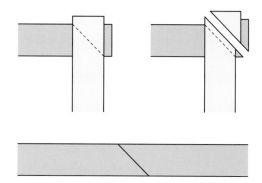

4. Add a label and a hanging sleeve, if desired.

5. Using laundry detergent and fabric softener, run your finished quilt through a normal cycle in your washer and dryer to fray the raw edges of the snowflake appliqués. If needed, trim away any long threads after drying.

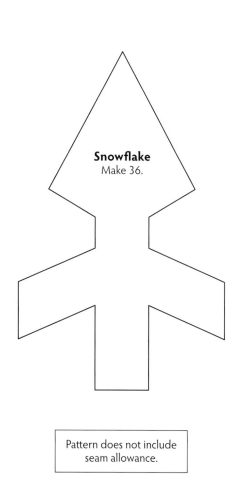

**Snowflake**
Make 36.

Pattern does not include seam allowance.

# JOY Wall Hanging

While in junior high, Claudia created a holiday display for her school's office that featured large candles made of cardboard tubes wrapped in red paper. Her mother reused those paper candles for many holiday seasons. Years later, Claudia's elementary-aged son made a small felt banner as a Christmas gift that featured the word *Joy*. Inspired by these memories, she created a quilt that combines the two elements.

Designed and made by Claudia L'Heureux Cole | Finished wall hanging: 25½" x 37"
Finished center block: 20½" x 23"

## Materials

*Yardage is based on 42"-wide fabric. Fat quarters measure 18" x 21".*

1 yard of floral print for borders and binding

⅜ yard of gray print for appliqué background

1 fat quarter of red print for candles

1 fat quarter of gold print for letters

5" x 6" piece of yellow print for flames

1 yard of fabric for backing

32" x 43" piece of batting

12" x 16" piece of paper-backed fusible web

## Cutting

**From the floral print, cut:**

2 rectangles, 8½" x 23½"

2 strips, 1½" x 37"

4 strips, 2¼" x 42"

**From the gray print, cut:**

1 strip, 3½" x 42"; crosscut into 2 strips, 3½" x 21"

1 strip, 3" x 42"; crosscut into 2 strips, 3" x 21"

1 strip, 4½" x 24"; crosscut into:

    1 rectangle, 4½" x 6"

    1 rectangle, 4½" x 7"

    1 rectangle, 4½" x 8"

**From the red print, cut:**

1 rectangle, 4½" x 15½"

1 rectangle, 4½" x 14½"

1 rectangle, 4½" x 13½"

## Making the Center Block

1. Sew the red 4½" x 15½" rectangle to the gray 4½" x 6" rectangle to make the center candle. Sew the red 4½" x 14½" rectangle to the gray 4½" x 7" rectangle to make the right candle. Sew the red 4½" x 13½" rectangle to the gray 4½" x 8" rectangle to make the left candle. Press all of the seam allowances toward the red.

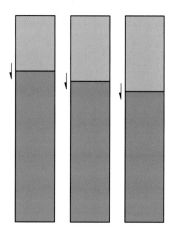

2. Sew the gray 3"-wide strips to the sides of the middle candle. Sew the left candle to the left side of the sewn strips and the right candle to the right side of the sewn strips. Add a gray

3½"-wide strip to each side to complete the center block. Press all seam allowances toward the gray strips.

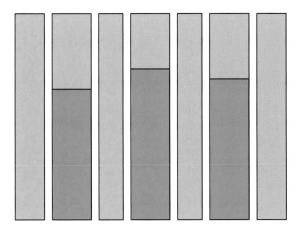

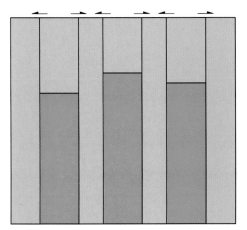

## Appliquéing the Letters and Flames

Using the patterns (pages 16 and 17), trace the *J*, *O*, *Y*, and three candle flames onto the paper side of the fusible web. Cut out the shapes, leaving ¼" around the traced lines. To make the letters, follow the manufacturer's instructions to press the fusible web to the wrong side of the gold fabric. Cut out the letters on the traced line. Referring to the quilt photo (page 13) and to "Fusing JOY," above right, for letter placement, fuse the letters to one of the floral-print 8½" x 23½" rectangles. Fuse the flames ⅜" above the center of each candle. Using a small zigzag stitch and matching thread, edgestitch all of the appliqués to secure.

### Fusing JOY

For letter placement, crease one of the floral-print 8½" x 23½" rectangles in half widthwise. Position the *O* so that it's centered on the crease and the bottom of the *O* is positioned 1" above the bottom raw edge of the rectangle. Arrange the *J* and *Y* to the sides of the *O*.

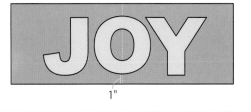

1"

## Assembling the Wall Hanging

Sew the *JOY* border rectangle to the top of the center block and the remaining floral-print 8½" x 23½" rectangle to the bottom. Press the seam allowances toward the border rectangles. Add the floral-print 1½"-wide strips to the sides and press the seam allowances toward the strips.

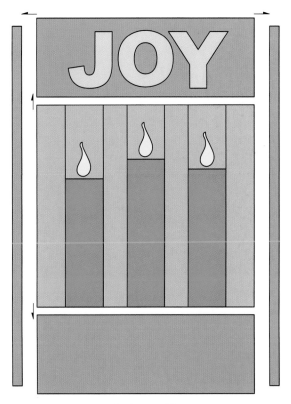

Quilt assembly

## Finishing the Wall Hanging

For help with any of the finishing steps, go to ShopMartingale.com/HowtoQuilt for free downloadable information.

1. Cut the backing fabric so it's 4" to 6" larger than the quilt top on all sides. Layer the quilt top, batting, and backing; baste the layers together.

2. Hand or machine quilt as desired.

3. Using the floral-print 2¼"-wide strips, prepare and sew the binding to the quilt.

4. Add a hanging sleeve and label, if desired.

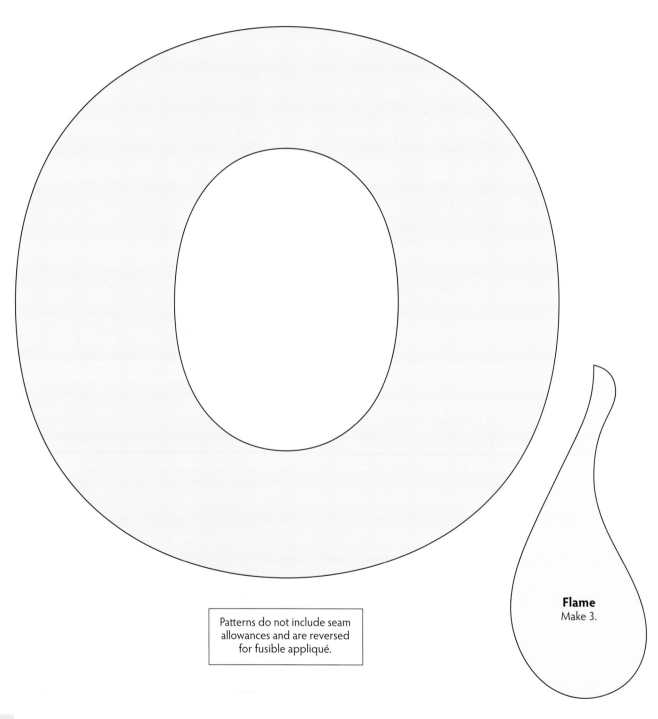

Patterns do not include seam allowances and are reversed for fusible appliqué.

**Flame**
Make 3.

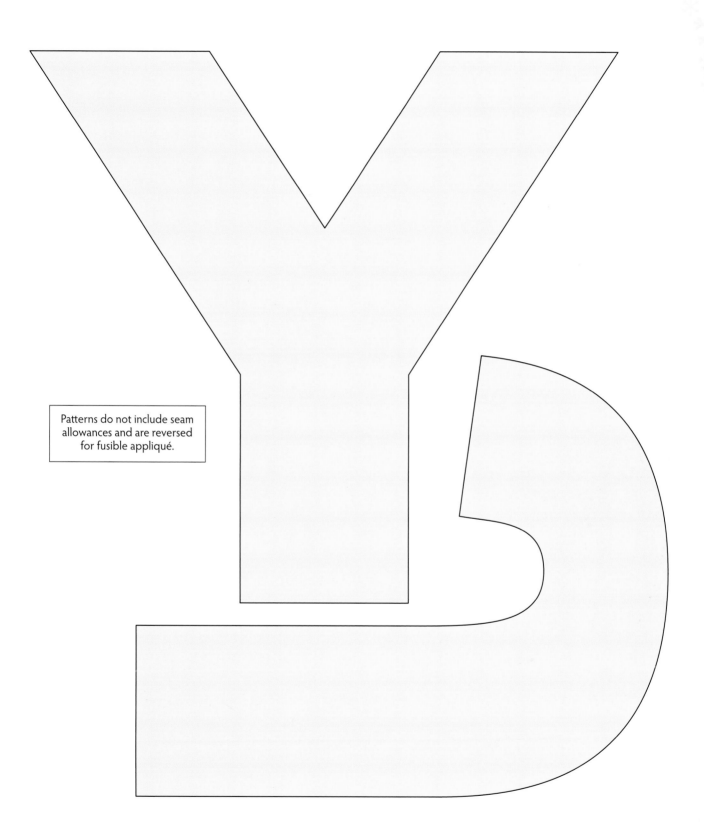

Patterns do not include seam allowances and are reversed for fusible appliqué.

# Ode to the Grinch Quilt

"And what happened then . . . ?
Well . . . in *Who*-ville they say
That the Grinch's small heart
Grew three sizes that day!"
~From *How the Grinch Stole Christmas* by Dr. Seuss

Stitch a wacky, wild Christmas quilt for a special boy or girl with none other than the Grinch as your muse. Pair the quilt with a copy of *How the Grinch Stole Christmas* for a great gift that will make a little one's heart grow three sizes on Christmas day!

| Designed, pieced, and quilted by Jenny Wilding Cardon | Finished quilt: 60½" x 60½"<br>Finished block: 12" x 12" |
| --- | --- |

## Materials

*Yardage is based on 40"-wide flannel. Jenny used the Moda Marbles fabric line.*

3¾ yards of mottled-red flannel for blocks, appliqué, and binding

3¼ yards of mottled-lime flannel for blocks

4¼ yards of fabric for backing

66" x 66" piece of batting

Washable glue stick

12½" x 12½" rotary-cutting ruler (optional)

6½" x 6½" rotary-cutting ruler (optional)

## Cutting

**From the mottled-red flannel, cut:**

32 strips, 3" x 13¼"

144 strips, 1½" x 7½"

7 strips, 2" x 40"

Reserve the remaining red flannel for appliqué.

**From the mottled-lime flannel, cut:**

31 strips, 3" x 13¼"

144 strips, 1½" x 7½"

8 squares, 12½" x 12½"

## Making the Striped Blocks

1. Lay out four red and three lime 3" x 13¼" strips horizontally in front of you. On the *left* raw edge of each of the red strips, mark a dot 1¼"

from the top. On the *right* raw edge of the lime strips, mark a dot 1¼" from the top.

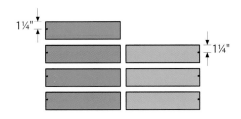

2. Place a lime strip on top of a red strip, right sides together, with dots on opposite edges. Position the top-*left* corner of the lime strip so it touches the dot on the red strip. Position the top-*right* corner of the lime strip so it touches the top-right corner of the red strip. Sew across the top edge of the lime strip using a ¼" seam allowance. Trim away the excess red fabric, leaving a ¼" seam allowance. Open and press the seam allowances toward the top.

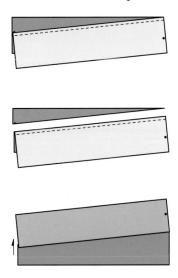

3. Repeat step 2 to sew a red strip to the lime strip, but position the top-*right* corner of the red strip so it touches the dot on the lime strip and the top-*left* corner so it touches the top-left corner of the lime strip. Continue adding strips in this manner, alternating sides and colors, until you have sewn together all seven strips from step 1. Square up the block to 12½" x 12½", angling your rotary ruler as needed to include at least ½" of the top and bottom horizontal strips. Make five blocks that begin and end with a red strip.

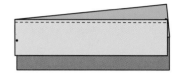

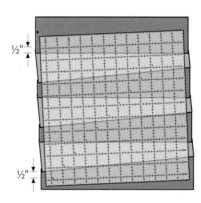

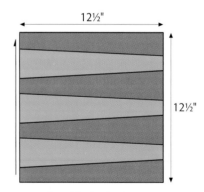

Make 5 blocks that begin and end with a red strip.

4. Repeat steps 1–3 to make four blocks that begin and end with a *lime* strip (you'll need four lime strips and three red strips for each block). To do this, mark a dot 1¼" from the top on the *left* raw edge of the *lime* strips. On the *right* raw edge of the *red* strips, mark a dot 1¼" from the top.

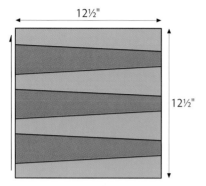

Make 4 blocks that begin and end with a lime strip.

### Which Edge of the Strip Am I Marking?

For odd-numbered strips (strips 1, 3, 5, and 7), dots will always be on the left. For even-numbered strips (2, 4, and 6), dots will always be on the right.

5. Repeat steps 1–3 to make the small strip quarter-blocks, but use the red and lime 1½" x 7½" strips instead. You'll need nine total strips for these quarter-blocks (five strips of one color and four strips of the other color). Also, when you mark the dots on the left and right raw edges of the strips, mark them just ¾" from the top. Square up the quarter-blocks to 6½" x 6½", angling your rotary ruler as needed to include at least ¼" of the top and bottom horizontal strips. Make 16 quarter-blocks that begin and end with a red strip and 16 quarter-blocks that begin and

end with a lime strip. Open and press the seam allowances toward the top.

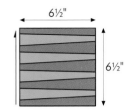

Make 16 blocks that begin and end with a red strip.

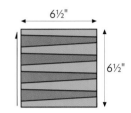

Make 16 blocks that begin and end with a lime strip.

6. Referring to the quilt photo (page 18), lay out two quarter-blocks that begin with a red strip and two that begin with a lime strip as shown. Sew two rows of two quarter-blocks each and press the seam allowances as indicated by the arrows. Join the rows to complete one Striped Four Patch block. Press the seam allowances open to reduce bulk. Make eight blocks.

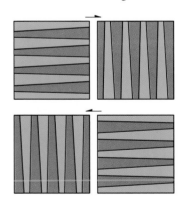

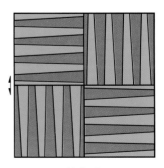

Make 8.

## Making the Heart Blocks

1. Trace the four heart patterns (pages 22–24) onto cardstock (a bright or light or window behind the patterns make this easier) and cut them out. Place the heart patterns *right* side up on the *wrong* side of the remaining red flannel and trace, leaving at least ½" of space between shapes. Trace the number of hearts listed on each pattern. Cut out the flannel shapes just inside the drawn lines.

2. Center a small heart on a lime 12½" square. Dab the wrong side of the heart with a glue stick to keep it in place for raw-edge appliqué. Use a machine straight stitch and matching thread to sew. Topstitch ¼" from the raw edge to secure the heart in place. If you wish, cut away the background fabric behind the heart, leaving a ¼" seam allowance. Jenny kept the background fabric intact in her quilt to add more dimension to the blocks. Make two blocks.

Make 2.

3. Make six more Heart blocks. The medium Heart blocks use small and medium hearts stacked as shown. The large Heart blocks use

three stacked hearts and the extra-large Heart blocks use four stacked hearts. Make two of each block.

Make 2 of each.

## Assembling the Quilt Top

Using the quilt photo (page 18) for placement and orientation, lay out the blocks in five rows of five blocks each. Sew the blocks into rows and press the seam allowances in opposite directions from row to row. Sew the rows together and press the seam allowances open to reduce bulk.

## Finishing the Quilt

For help with any of the finishing steps, go to ShopMartingale.com/HowtoQuilt for free downloadable information.

1. Cut the backing fabric so it's 4" to 6" larger than the quilt top on all sides. Layer the quilt top, batting, and backing; baste the layers together.

2. Hand or machine quilt as desired.

3. Square up the quilt sandwich.

4. Using the red 2"-wide strips, prepare and sew the binding to the quilt. Add a label and a hanging sleeve, if desired.

5. Using laundry detergent and fabric softener, run your finished quilt through a normal cycle in your washer and dryer to fray the raw edges of the heart appliqués. Trim away any long threads after drying, if needed.

Pattern does not include seam allowances and is reversed for raw-edge appliqué.

**Medium heart**
Make 6.

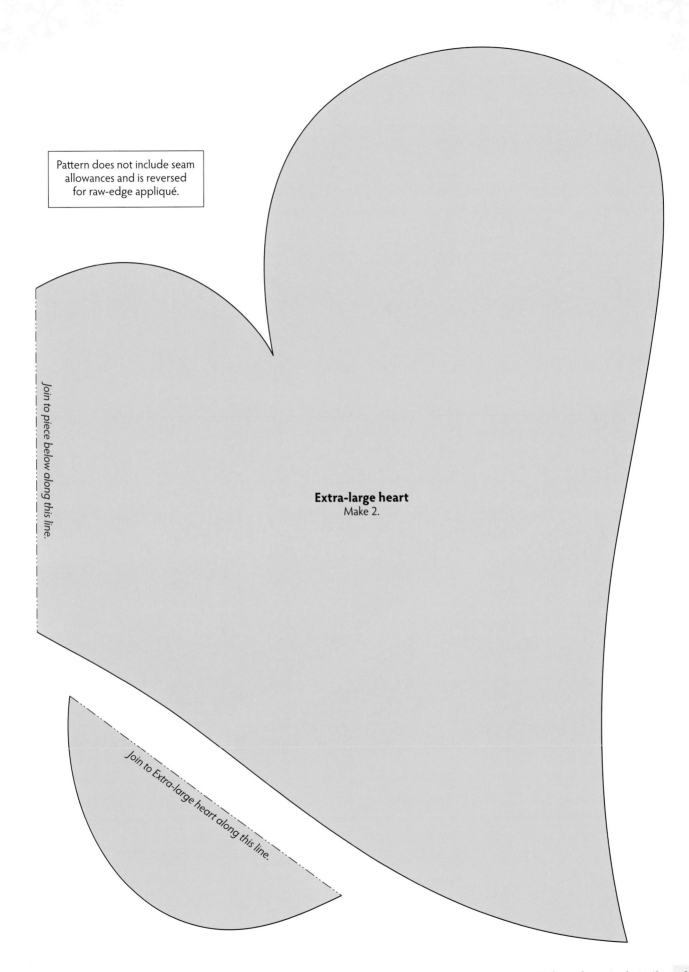

Pattern does not include seam allowances and is reversed for raw-edge appliqué.

Join to piece below along this line.

**Extra-large heart**
Make 2.

Join to Extra-large heart along this line.

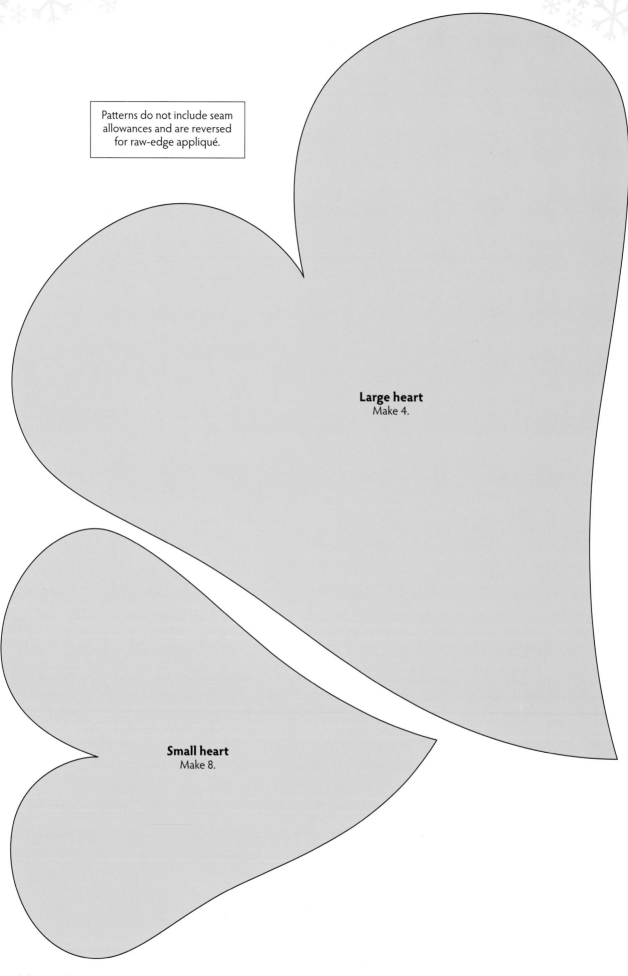

Patterns do not include seam allowances and are reversed for raw-edge appliqué.

**Large heart**
Make 4.

**Small heart**
Make 8.

# There's Snow One Else for Me Wall Hanging

W hen Tiffany first discovered Snowball blocks, she immediately thought of building a snowman with them. This wall hanging was inspired by a wooden cutout that Tiffany and her husband had at their winter wedding. It makes a sweet Christmas accent piece and doubles as an anniversary decoration for them in January!

Designed and pieced by Tiffany Mottet; quilted by Diana Scott | Finished wall hanging: 20½" x 32½"
Finished block: 8" x 8"

## Materials

*Yardage is based on 42"-wide fabric. Fat quarters measure 18" x 21".*

⅝ yard of blue print for Snowball blocks, background, and binding

½ yard of white fabric for Snowball blocks*

¼ yard of mottled-gray fabric for top and bottom borders

1 fat quarter of black fabric for letters and hat

Scraps of red, mottled-red, green, and orange fabrics for appliqués

1⅛ yards of fabric for backing and hanging sleeve

27" x 39" piece of batting

4 black buttons, ⅞" diameter, for eyes

Assorted red buttons for necklace

16"-long piece of black super-bulky yarn for arms

1 yard of 17"-wide paper-backed fusible web

Pigma pen, black

*Tiffany used a white fabric with silver glitter printed on it to add sparkle to the Snowball blocks.*

## Cutting

**From the blue print, cut:**

6 strips, 2½" x 42"; crosscut *3 of the strips* into:
    2 strips, 2½" x 24½"
    2 rectangles, 2½" x 8½"
    16 squares, 2½" x 2½"
1 strip, 1½" x 42"; crosscut into:
    8 squares, 1½" x 1½"
    4 rectangles, 1½" x 6½"

**From the white fabric, cut:**

1 strip, 8½" x 42"; crosscut into 4 squares, 8½" x 8½"
1 strip, 6½" x 14"; crosscut into 2 squares, 6½" x 6½"

**From the mottled-gray fabric, cut:**

1 strip, 4½" x 42"; crosscut into 2 strips, 4½" x 20½"

## Making the Blocks

1. Draw a diagonal line from corner to corner on the wrong side of each blue 2½" square. Place a marked square on one corner of a white 8½" square, right sides together and raw edges aligned. Sew on the marked line. Trim the excess corner fabric, leaving a ¼" seam allowance. Flip the corner triangle open and press the seam allowances toward the blue triangle. Repeat on the remaining three corners of the white square to complete one Snowball block. Make four blocks.

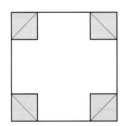 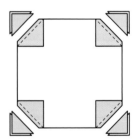

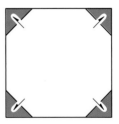

Make 4.

2. Repeat step 1 using the blue 1½" squares and the white 6½" squares to make two small snowball units.

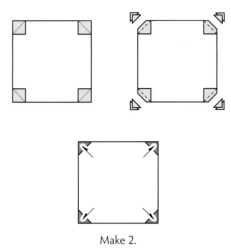

Make 2.

3. Sew the blue 1½" x 6½" rectangles to opposite sides of each unit from step 2. Press the seam allowances toward the rectangles. Sew a blue 2½" x 8½" rectangle to the top of each unit. Press the seam allowances toward the blue rectangles. The units should measure 8½" x 8½".

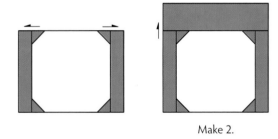

Make 2.

## Assembling the Wall-Hanging Center

1. Arrange the blocks in three rows of two blocks each as shown. Sew the blocks together in rows, pressing the seam allowances in opposite directions from row to row. Join the rows. Press the seam allowances toward the bottom of the wall hanging.

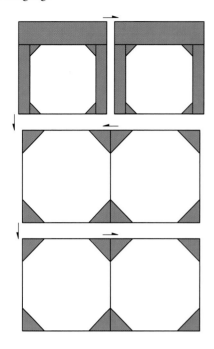

2. Sew the blue 2½" x 24½" strips to the sides of the quilt center. Press the seam allowances toward the strips. Sew a gray 20½"-long strip to the top of the wall hanging. Press the seam allowances toward the strip.

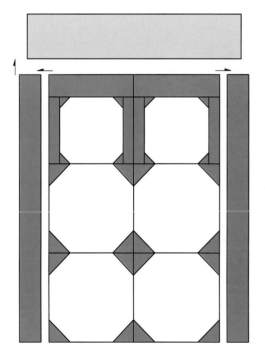

## Appliquéing the Wall Hanging

1. Cut the black yarn into two strands, each about 6½" long. Referring to the photo (page 25) for placement, position the yarn for the arms. Use black thread to hand sew the yarn in place using a couching stitch and add a few satin stitches at the ends to secure.

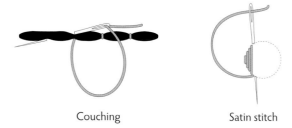

Couching          Satin stitch

2. Trace the patterns (pages 29–31) onto the paper side of the fusible web. Cut out the letters and shapes, leaving ¼" around the traced line. Following the manufacturer's instructions, press the fusible web to the wrong side of the black fabric and assorted scraps. Cut out the appliqué letters and shapes on the traced line. **Note:** Since the letter appliqués are particularly small, use finely-pointed scissors to make sharp points and cut-out centers.

3. Referring to the photo for placement, arrange the letter appliqués on the remaining gray 20½"-long strip. Fuse the appliqués in place, and then edge-stitch each letter with matching thread and a machine zigzag or blanket stitch to secure.

4. Sew the appliquéd strip to the bottom of the quilt center. Press the seam allowances toward the strip.

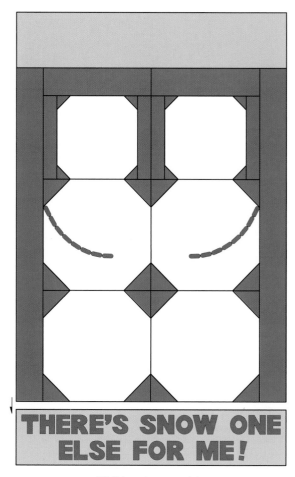

Wall-hanging assembly

5. Arrange the remaining appliqués on the wall-hanging top and fuse in place. Edgestitch each shape with matching thread and a machine zigzag or blanket stitch to secure.

## Finishing the Wall Hanging

For help with any of the finishing steps, go to ShopMartingale.com/HowtoQuilt for free downloadable information.

1. Add the black buttons for the eyes on both snowpeople and add the assorted red buttons for the necklace on the snowwoman.

2. Using the Pigma pen, draw dots for the smiles.

3. Cut the backing fabric so it's 4" to 6" larger than the wall-hanging top on all sides. Layer the top, batting, and backing; baste the layers together. Quilt as desired. Diana echo quilted the Snowball blocks and appliqué shapes and quilted along each seam.

4. Add a hanging sleeve using leftover fabric from the backing.

5. Using the remaining blue 2½"-wide strips, prepare and sew the binding to the quilt. Add a label, if desired.

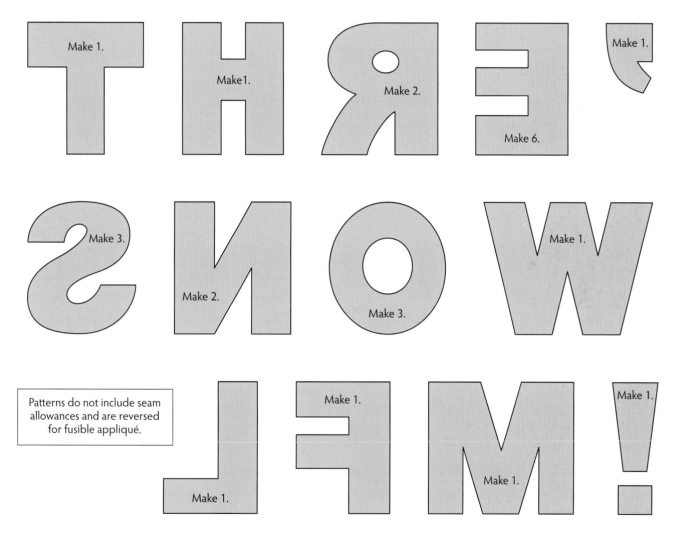

Patterns do not include seam allowances and are reversed for fusible appliqué.

**Letters**
Make the number of letters given from black fabric.

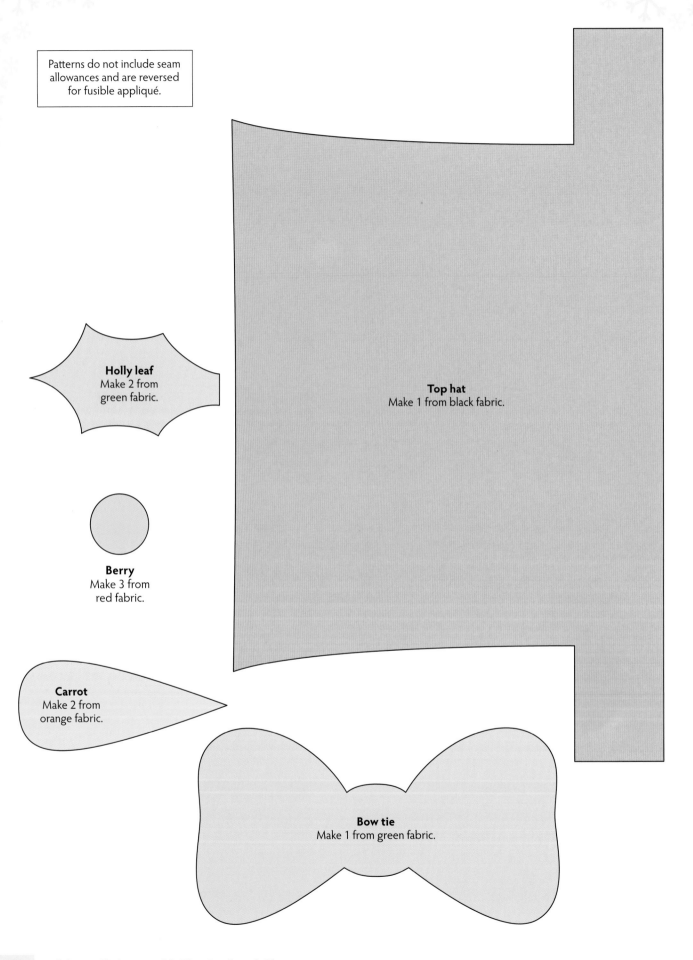

Patterns do not include seam allowances and are reversed for fusible appliqué.

**Holly leaf**
Make 2 from green fabric.

**Top hat**
Make 1 from black fabric.

**Berry**
Make 3 from red fabric.

**Carrot**
Make 2 from orange fabric.

**Bow tie**
Make 1 from green fabric.

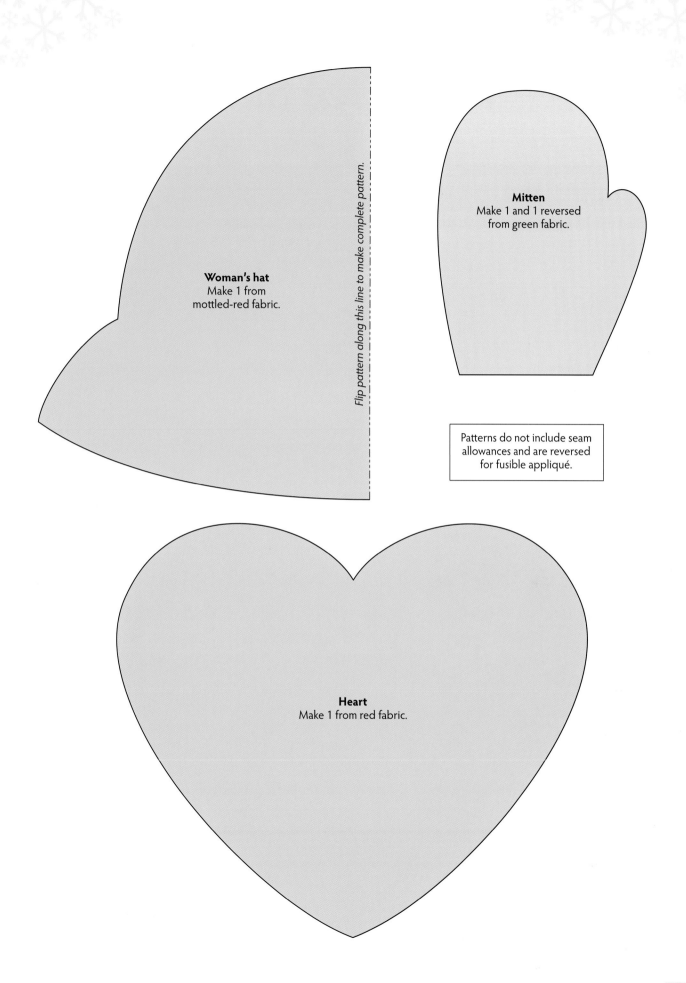

**Woman's hat**
Make 1 from
mottled-red fabric.

Flip pattern along this line to make complete pattern.

**Mitten**
Make 1 and 1 reversed
from green fabric.

Patterns do not include seam
allowances and are reversed
for fusible appliqué.

**Heart**
Make 1 from red fabric.

# Tulle Tree Skirt

A fun, pointed tree skirt that's stylish enough for both you and your tree! You can use coordinating prints as shown, all one colorway, or a different print for each leaf to suit your style. You can even use sparkly tulle or tulle with an embossed texture!

Designed and made by Diane Chin | Finished tree skirt: 22" x 32"

## Materials

*Yardage is based on 42"-wide fabric unless otherwise noted.*

4 yards of 44"-wide white tulle for skirt

2¼ yards of red print for leaves

1 yard of green polka dot for leaves

⅝ yard of green plaid for leaves

⅝ yard of green candy print for leaves

2 yards of ½"-wide red grosgrain ribbon for tie

## Cutting

*Join the pattern pieces on pages 34 and 35 to make a complete leaf template.*

**From the red print, cut:**
16 leaf shapes

**From the green polka dot, cut:**
6 leaf shapes

**From the green plaid, cut:**
4 leaf shapes

**From the green candy print, cut:**
4 leaf shapes

## Assembling the Leaves

1. Sew two matching leaf shapes right sides together using a ¼" seam allowance; leave the flat end open. Turn right side out and use an iron to press flat. Using a zigzag stitch, machine stitch across the top open end of each leaf. Repeat to make 15 leaves total.

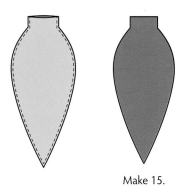

Make 15.

2. Lay out the eight red leaves side by side with top edges aligned. Adjust spacing so the total width of the row is 32". Pin the leaves together, and then machine baste across their top edges to secure.

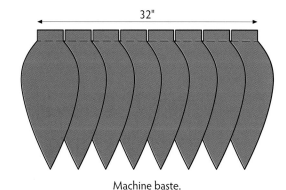

32"

Machine baste.

3. Fold under ¾" along the flat edge of each green leaf. Position the green leaves on top of the red leaves, placing each green leaf halfway between two red leaves and with the folded edge over

the top of the red leaves. Pin in place, and then topstitch ⅝" from the folded edges to form a casing.

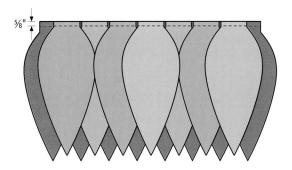

one end of the ribbon and use it to thread the ribbon through the leaf casing.

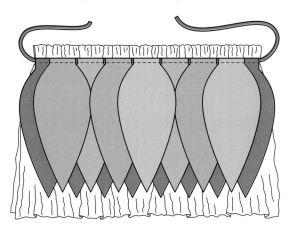

## Assembling the Tree Skirt

1. Fold the tulle in half widthwise so it's 22" wide. Sew a long basting stitch along the length of the tulle, 2½" from the fold, and then gather the tulle along the basting thread until the tulle measures 32" in length.

2. Position the leaves on top of the tulle so the topstitching line of the leaf casing is aligned with the tulle's basting thread. Approximately 1¾" of the folded tulle will show above the tops of the leaves. Sew along the topstitching through all layers. Attach a safety pin to

### Handling the Ribbon Ends

Trim each end of the ribbon at a 45° angle to prevent fraying. If you still experience fraying, dab the ends with Fray Check or clear nail polish and their raveling days will be over!

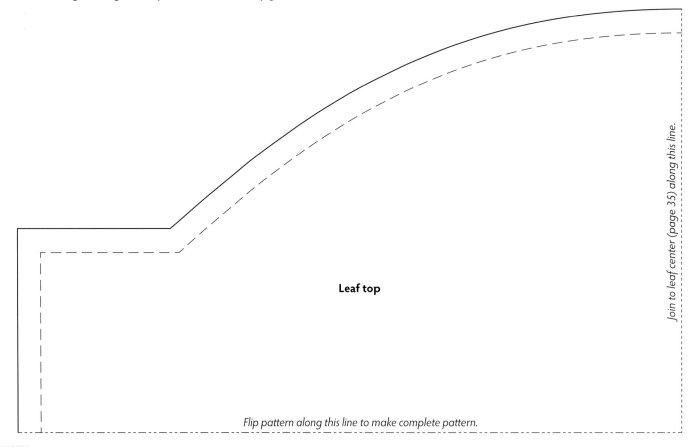

Join to leaf center (page 35) along this line.

**Leaf top**

*Flip pattern along this line to make complete pattern.*

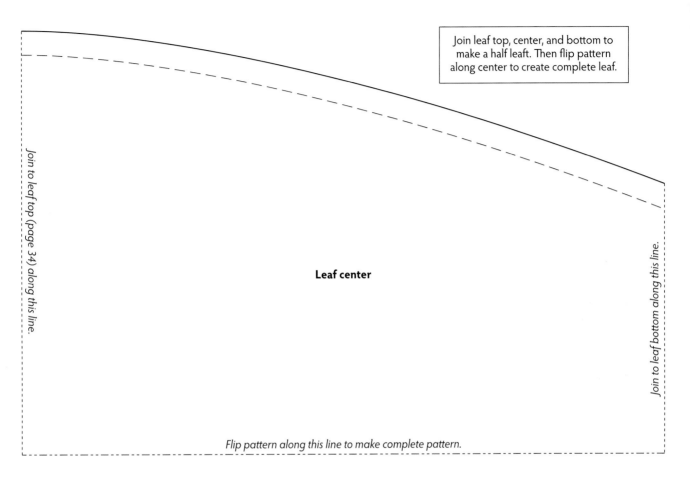

Join leaf top, center, and bottom to make a half leaft. Then flip pattern along center to create complete leaf.

*Join to leaf top (page 34) along this line.*

**Leaf center**

*Join to leaf bottom along this line.*

*Flip pattern along this line to make complete pattern.*

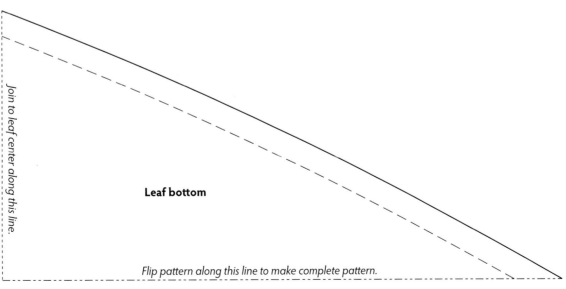

*Join to leaf center along this line.*

**Leaf bottom**

*Flip pattern along this line to make complete pattern.*

# Dotty for Christmas
# Tree Skirt

Karen's crazy for circles, dotty for dots, wild about whirls. So it's no surprise that her project includes circles! Lots of them. This fun and easy project can be made in any color combination you're using for your holiday decorating. Karen loves the bright colors popular for Christmas ornaments at the moment, so her tree skirt is packed with happy, festive colors.

| Designed and pieced by Karen Morrell Johnson; quilted by Molly Hanson | Finished tree skirt: 54" diameter |
| --- | --- |

## Materials

*Yardage is based on 42"-wide fabric. Fat quarters measure 18" x 21".*

4⅛ yards of aqua solid for skirt background and bias binding

1 fat quarter *each* of red, magenta, green #1, green #2, and white fabrics

3⅜ yards of fabric for backing*

60" square of batting

2 yards of 17"-wide paper-backed fusible web

32" piece of nonstretchy yarn, cord, or selvage for marking circle shapes

Matching ribbon for ties (optional)

*Yardage is sufficient for a backing with one seam. If you're creative with your piecing, you can use less.*

## Cutting

**From the aqua solid, cut:**

2 rectangles, 28" x 55"

2"-wide bias-cut strips to total 185"

## Assembling the Skirt Background

1. With right sides together and using a ¼" seam allowance, sew the two aqua rectangles together along a 55" edge to create a large square. Press the seam allowances open to reduce bulk.

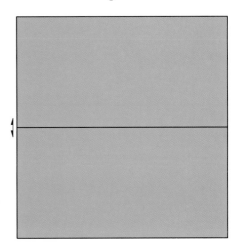

2. Fold the square in half, and then in half again, forming a folded square with four layers. Lay the folded square on a large, flat surface and smooth gently.

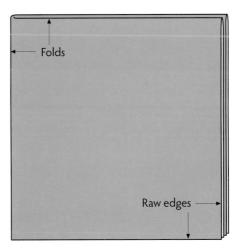

3. Tie a marking pen to one end of a 32"-long piece of nonstretchy yarn, cord, or even a selvage strip. Measure 27½" from the pen, and then tape that point of the yarn to the folded corner of the square. Check to make sure that the distance between the corner and the pen is 27½", making adjustments if necessary. Carefully keeping the pen in an upright position, mark a quarter circle on the square.

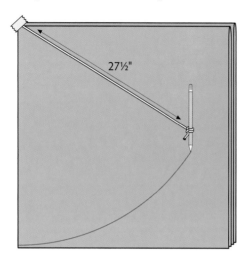

27½"

4. Using scissors, cut through all four layers on the drawn line.

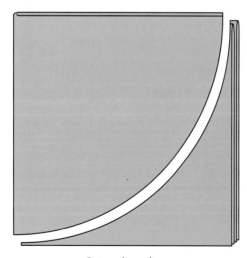

Cut on drawn line.

5. Repeat this process to create the center hole, changing the yarn measurement between the tape and the pen to 2½". Mark the quarter circle and cut on the line.

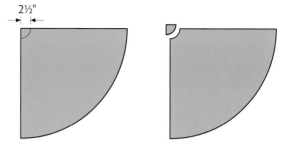

2½"

6. Open the newly cut circle and press gently to remove creases.

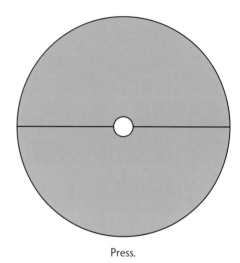

Press.

## Appliquéing the Dots

1. Using the dot patterns (pages 40), trace the number of each pattern as listed below for one color onto the paper side of the fusible web, leaving 1/4" between the traced dots. Following the manufacturer's instructions, press the fusible web to the wrong side of the appropriate fabric. Cut out the dots on the traced lines. Repeat for each color.

   **Red:** two A, two B, four C, and six D dots

   **Magenta:** two A, three B, five C, and six D dots

   **Green #1:** two A, one B, two C, and eight D dots

   **Green #2:** two A, two B, four C, and seven D dots

   **White:** three B, three C, and 40 E dots

### Fusing a Large Appliqué Project

Before you fuse any of the dots, you should audition the entire layout. Use a surface large enough for the entire circle to lie flat, like a large table or the floor. Lay out *all* of the dots, and then use a digital camera to photograph the arrangement. If you aren't satisfied with what you see, then rearrange the dots until you have an arrangement you like in the photo. When you're ready to fuse the dots in place, slide a flat, portable ironing board under the skirt to protect the table or floor. Fuse one small section of dots at a time by keeping the skirt still, but moving the flat board from spot to spot. After everything is fused, you can safely pick up the skirt without losing any dots.

2. Place the aqua circle on a large, flat surface. Arrange and rearrange the prepared dots on it until you have an arrangement you like. Fuse all the dots in place.

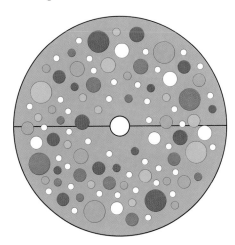

3. Appliqué the edges using your favorite method. Karen layered her circle with batting and backing first, and then used a free-motion straight stitch to stitch ⅛" inside each dot's edge to secure the dot in place. She left the edges raw and stitched through all of the layers, appliquéing the dots and quilting the tree skirt at the same time.

## Finishing the Tree Skirt

For help with any of the finishing steps, go to ShopMartingale.com/HowtoQuilt for free downloadable information.

1. Layer the skirt top, batting, and backing; baste the layers together. Quilt as desired.

2. Trim the layers on both the inside and outside circle edges, cutting away the excess batting and backing.

### Avoiding bias distortion

Dealing with bias edges on both the top and the backing of a circular project while quilting can distort the circle and make it ripple. To avoid this, piece the backing into a rectangle or square. (For the tree skirt, piece a 60" square.) Then layer the batting and circle on top of it, baste, and then quilt as desired. Do not trim the backing into a circle until the quilting is complete.

3. Avoiding the seams, choose a favorite side of the skirt to be the front. On the opposite side, cut a straight line from the outer edge to the inner circle opening to create a back opening.

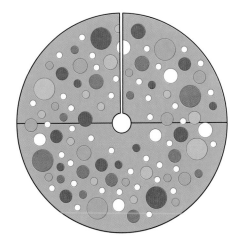

4. Use the aqua 2"-wide bias strips to make the binding. Bind all of the edges of the tree skirt, including the outer circle, the edges of the cut opening, and the inner circle.

5. Optional: hand stitch ribbons at the top, bottom, and middle of the straight edges to create ties. Add a label, if desired.

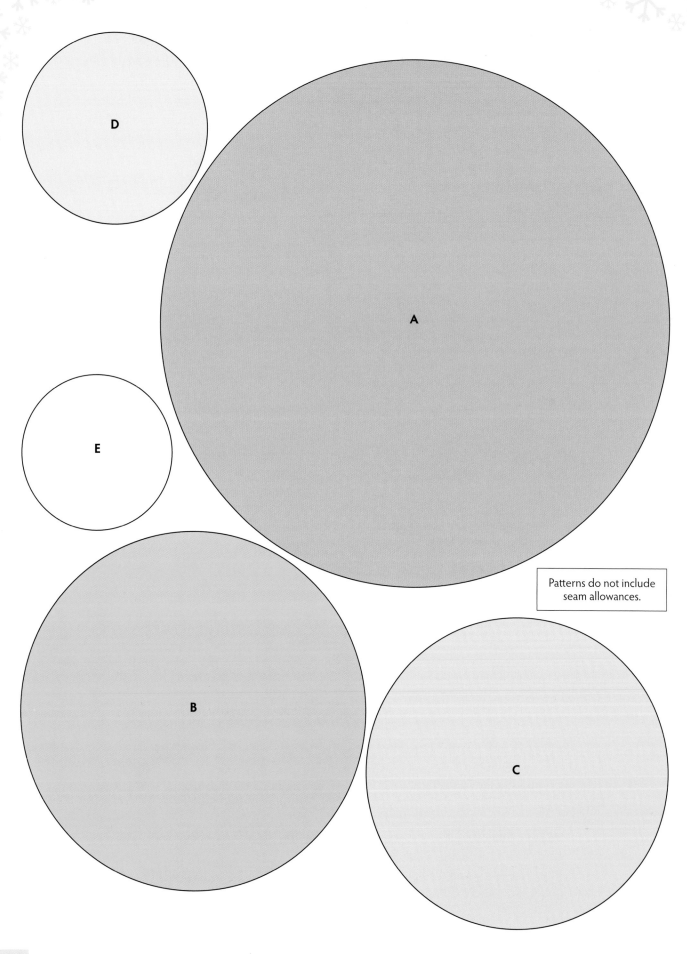

D

A

E

Patterns do not include
seam allowances.

B

C

# Paper Chains
# Table Runner

Colorful construction-paper chains are cheerful reminders of childhood and our earliest, often clumsy, attempts at arts and crafts. A Christmas tree festooned with strings of linked paper rings—simple, inexpensive, handmade—was the inspiration for this bright and easy table runner.

| Designed and made by Mary V. Green; machine quilted by Molly Hanson | Finished table runner: 18" x 60" |
| --- | --- |

## Materials

*Yardage is based on 42"-wide fabric unless otherwise noted.*

2 yards of gold print for background and backing

⅓ yard of red print for binding

10" x 10" square *each* of 9 assorted fabrics for rings

24" x 66" piece of batting

1⅜ yards of 18"-wide paper-backed fusible web

## Cutting

**From the *lengthwise* grain of the gold print, cut:**
2 strips, 20" x 62"

**From the red print, cut:**
4 strips, 2¼" x 42"

## Appliquéing the Table Runner

1.  To make arranging the rings easier, mark the shape of the table runner on one gold strip in the following manner. On the right side of the fabric, measure and mark an 18" x 60" rectangle, centering it on the gold strip. On both ends of the drawn rectangle, measure 11" from the corners on each long side and 9" from the corners on each short side; draw a line between the marks as shown to indicate the pointed ends.

Measure and mark
the background fabric.

2.  Prepare nine rings using the ring pattern (page 43), fusible web, and the 10" squares. One half of the ring pattern is provided; to make a template, trace the pattern onto a folded sheet of paper and cut it out. Open the paper and use the template to trace the rings onto the paper side of the fusible web. Cut out the rings, leaving ¼" around the traced lines. Following the manufacturer's instructions, press the fusible web to the wrong side of the assorted 10" squares. Cut out the rings on the traced line.

3.  Using a rotary cutter or scissors, make a single cut through each ring as shown. Peel off the paper backing but do not fuse anything yet.

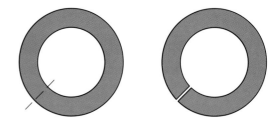

4.  Arrange the rings on the background fabric, playing with the order and placement until you're pleased with the result. Use the cut slits to link the rings together, rotating the rings as needed to make sure the cut edges are covered by an adjacent ring.

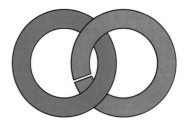

Link rings together as shown.

5.  When you're satisfied with the placement of the rings, fuse them in place. If you wish, secure the rings further with invisible machine appliqué.

## Finishing the Table Runner

For help with any of the finishing steps, go to ShopMartingale.com/HowtoQuilt for free downloadable information.

1. Layer the table-runner top with the batting and backing. Baste the layers together.

2. Hand or machine quilt as desired.

3. Trim the edges of the runner along the marked lines.

4. Using the red-print strips, prepare and sew the binding to the quilt.

Patterns do not include seam allowances.

*Place on fold.*

*Place on fold.*

**Ring**
*Make 9.*

# Festival of Lights
# Table Runner

Everyone enjoys lighting the candles at Hanukkah. No matter which side of the table you're sitting on, you can "light" the candles on this cheerful menorah each night of Hanukkah. Family and friends will enjoy celebrating the holiday with you. And they'll all want a table runner of their own!

Designed and pieced by Tracy Overturf; quilted by Lynn Reppas; buttonholes by Jane Ellwood

Finished table runner: 20½" x 35"

## Materials

*Yardage is based on 42"-wide fabric.*

½ yard of white print for background

⅜ yard of Hanukkah print for center candle and border

14" x 20" piece of gold felted wool for flames

4 strips, 2½" x 15", of different blue prints for candles

¼ yard of blue dot for binding

1⅓ yards of fabric for backing

26" x 42" piece of batting

18 buttons, ⅝" diameter

## Cutting

**From the white print, cut:**

2 strips, 1½" x 42"; crosscut into:
    6 strips, 1½" x 6½"
    2 strips, 1½" x 8½"
4 rectangles, 5½" x 11½"
2 squares, 4½" x 4½"
2 strips, 3½" x 16½"

**From the Hanukkah print, cut:**

2 strips, 2½" x 42"
2 strips, 2½" x 42"; crosscut into:
    2 strips, 2½" x 26"
    1 strip, 2½" x 8½"

**From each of the blue strips, cut:**

2 strips, 2½" x 6½" (8 total)

**From the blue dot, cut:**

3 strips, 2¼" x 42"

## Assembling the Table Runner

1. Lay out the blue 6½"-long strips and the Hanukkah print 8½"-long strip so the 8½" strip representing the shamus candle is in the middle as shown. Arrange the blue strips so that the first strips on each side match, the second strips on each side match, and so on.

2. Sew white 6½"-long strips to the *right* sides of the first three blue strips on the left and to the *left* sides of the last three blue strips on the right to make six candle units. Press the seam allowances toward the blue strips.

3. Stitch together the three candle units from the left side in order, and then add the remaining blue strip as shown to complete the left candle set. In the reverse order, sew together the three candle units from the right side, and then add the remaining blue strip as shown to complete the right candle set. Press the seam allowances toward the blue strips.

4. Sew a white 5½" x 11½" strip to the top and bottom of each candle set. Press the seam allowances toward the rectangles

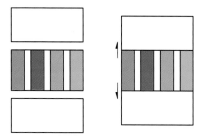

5. Sew a white 8½"-long strip to each side of the Hanukkah print 8½"-long strip. Press the seam allowances toward the center. Sew the white 4½" squares to the top and bottom to complete the center candle unit. Press the seam allowances toward the squares.

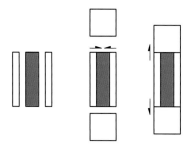

6. Sew the left and right candle units to the center candle unit. Press the seam allowances toward

the side units. Sew a white 16½"-long strip to each end. Press the seam allowances toward the strips.

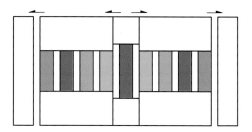

7. Measure the length of the table runner and cut the two Hanukkah print 42"-long strips to that measurement. Sew them to the long sides of the table runner. Press the seam allowances toward the strips. Measure the width of the table runner and cut the two Hanukkah print 26"-long strips to that measurement. Sew them to the ends of the runner. Press the seam allowances toward the strips.

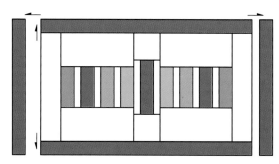

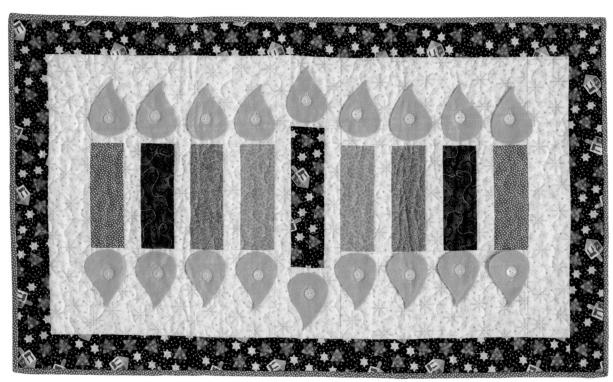

## Finishing the Table Runner

For help with any of the finishing steps, go to ShopMartingale.com/HowtoQuilt for free downloadable information.

1. Layer the table-runner top, batting, and backing; baste the layers together. Quilt as desired.

2. Using the blue-dot strips, prepare and sew the binding to the quilt.

## Making the Flames

1. Trace the flame pattern (below), including the buttonhole slit, onto cardstock (a bright light or window behind the template makes this easier) and cut it out. Cut the slit open. Use the cardstock template to trace 18 flames onto the gold wool. Use a pencil to mark the buttonholes through the slit.

2. Following the instructions in your sewing-machine manual and using gold thread, make a ⅝" buttonhole at each mark. Cut each buttonhole open, slightly smaller than needed. Cut each flame out just inside its drawn line.

3. Place a flame at the top of one of the candles on the table runner. Use a pencil to mark button placement through the buttonhole. Repeat to mark button placement on both ends of each candle. Using the marks as guides, sew the buttons to the table runner. Button the flames in place on each side of the table runner throughout the Festival of Lights.

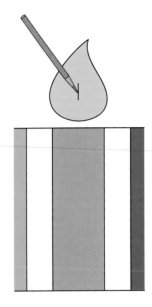

### Flame Keeper

Make a little bag to store the flames in until you need them. You could use one of your candle fabrics so your bag matches the table runner!

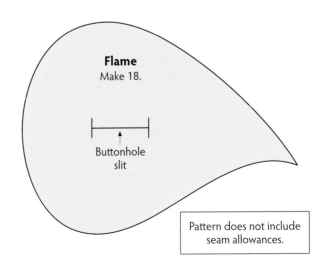

**Flame**
Make 18.

Buttonhole
slit

Pattern does not include
seam allowances.

# Christmas Twist-and-Turn Table Runner

This simple yet elegant table runner has built-in places in which to position a centerpiece or condiments. It looks lovely gracing your holiday table after the big dinner.

Designed and made by Leanne Clare | Finished table runner: 16½" x 58½"
Finished block: 3½" x 3½"

## Materials

*Yardage is based on 42"-wide fabric.*

1⅓ yards of mottled-cream fabric for blocks, border, and binding

½ yard of green Christmas print for blocks

½ yard of red Christmas print for blocks

1 yard of fabric for backing*

21" x 63" piece of batting

*To avoid a seam in the backing, purchase 2 yards of fabric.*

## Cutting

**From the mottled-cream fabric, cut:**

3 strips, 4⅜" x 42"; crosscut into 22 squares, 4⅜" x 4⅜"

2 squares, 4¾" x 4¾"; cut into quarters diagonally to make 8 triangles

2 strips, 4" x 42"; crosscut into 12 squares, 4" x 4"

1 strip, 1½" x 42"; crosscut into 2 strips, 1½" x 14½"

3 strips, 1½" x 42"

4 strips, 2½" x 42"

**From the green Christmas print, cut:**

2 strips, 4⅜" x 42"; crosscut into 13 squares, 4⅜" x 4⅜". Cut 2 squares in half diagonally to make 4 triangles.

1 square, 4¾" x 4¾"; cut into quarters diagonally to make 4 triangles

**From the red Christmas print, cut:**

2 strips, 4⅜" x 42"; crosscut into 13 squares, 4⅜" x 4⅜". Cut 2 squares in half diagonally to make 4 triangles.

1 square, 4¾" x 4¾"; cut into quarters diagonally to make 4 triangles

## Assembling the Units

1. Draw a diagonal line from corner to corner on the wrong side of a cream 4⅜" square. Layer the square on a green 4⅜" square, right sides together, and stitch ¼" from the line on both sides. Cut the squares apart on the drawn line to make two half-square-triangle units. Press the seam allowances away from the cream triangles. Make a total of 22 green/cream half-square-triangle units. Repeat to make 22 red/cream half-square-triangle units.

Make 22.

Make 22.

2. Sew a green 4¾" quarter-square triangle and a cream 4¾" quarter-square triangle together as shown to make a triangle unit. Press the seam allowances away from the cream triangle. Sew a red 4⅜" triangle to the triangle unit to make a red triangle unit. Press the seam allowances toward the large triangle. Make four red triangle units.

Make 4.

3. Repeat step 3 with the red quarter-square triangles, the remaining cream quarter-square

triangles, and the green 4⅜" triangles to make four green triangle units.

Make 4.

## Assembling the Table Runner

1. Lay out the cream 4" squares and all the pre-pared units in 16 rows as shown. Sew the pieces together in rows, pressing the seam allowances in opposite directions from row to row. Sew the rows together. Press the seam allowances in one direction.

2. Sew the cream 14½"-long strips to the ends. Press the seam allowances toward the strips. Sew the remaining 1½"-wide cream strips end to end to make one continuous strip; press. From this strip, cut two 1½" x 58½" border strips and sew them to the sides of the table runner. Press the seam allowances toward the strips.

## Finishing the Table Runner

For help with any of the finishing steps, go to ShopMartingale.com/HowtoQuilt for free down-loadable information.

1. Cut two 21" x 32" rectangles from the length-wise grain of the backing fabric. Sew the two pieces together along the short edges; press the seam allowances open.

2. Layer the table-runner top, batting, and back-ing; baste the layers together.

3. Hand or machine quilt as desired.

4. Using the cream 2½"-wide strips, prepare and sew the binding to the table runner.

5. Add a label, if desired.

# Holiday Delight Table Runner

Choose a cute Christmas charm pack and this table runner goes together in a flash. This runner is great to make for a last-minute gift. It's really that easy!

Designed and made by Cathy Valentine Reitan | Finished table runner: 20" x 55"

## Materials

*Yardage is based on 42"-wide fabric unless otherwise noted.*

½ yard of diagonal stripe for outer border

⅜ yard of cream solid for inner border

20 squares, 5" x 5", of assorted Christmas prints*

⅓ yard of red print for binding

Scraps for appliqué circles (or leftover charm squares if using precuts)

1⅞ yards of fabric for backing

26" x 61" piece of batting

17"-wide paper-backed fusible web (optional)

*You can use a pack of precut Christmas charm squares or cut squares from scraps.*

## Cutting

**From the diagonal stripe, cut:**

3 strips, 3" x 42"

1 strip, 3" x 42"; crosscut into 2 strips, 3" x 15"

**From the cream solid, cut:**

3 strips, 2¾" x 42"

1 strip, 2¾" x 42"; crosscut into 2 strips, 2¾" x 15"

**From the red print, cut:**

4 strips, 2" x 42"

## Assembling the Table Runner

1. Lay out the 20 assorted 5" squares in two rows of 10 squares each, evenly distributing the light, medium, and dark squares. Sew the squares into rows, pressing the seam allowances in opposite directions for each row. Sew the rows together and press the seam allowances open to reduce bulk.

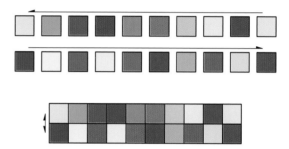

2. Sew the three cream 42"-long strips together end to end to make one continuous strip; press. From this strip, cut two 2¾" x 45½" border strips and sew them to the sides of the table runner. Press the seam allowances toward the strips. Sew the cream 15"-long strips to the ends; press the seam allowances toward the strips. Sew the striped 15"-long strips to the ends; press the seam allowances toward the strips. Sew the three striped 42"-long strips together end to end to make one continuous strip; press. From this strip, cut two 3" x 55" border strips and sew them to the sides of the table runner. Press the seam allowances toward the strips.

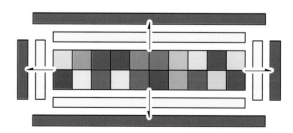

## Appliquéing the Circles

You may use any appliqué method to secure your circles to the table runner. Cathy used fusible appliqué, and then edgestitched each circle with a narrow machine satin stitch. Choose a variety of fabrics from your remaining charm squares or from your scrap basket. Using the pattern (below), cut 32 total circles from your fabrics. Lay out the circles on the cream border so they're evenly spaced and you're pleased with the arrangement. Appliqué the circles in place using your selected method.

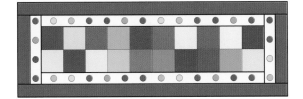

## Finishing the Table Runner

For help with any of the finishing steps, go to ShopMartingale.com/HowtoQuilt for free downloadable information.

1. Layer the table-runner top, batting, and backing.

2. Quilt as desired. Cathy quilted a spiral swirl in each of the charm squares and stitched ¼" from the seams in the cream border. In the striped border, she quilted a straight line on each green diagonal line.

3. Using the red 2"-wide strips, prepare and sew the binding to the table runner.

4. Add a label, if desired.

**Circle**
Make 32.

Pattern does not include
seam allowances.

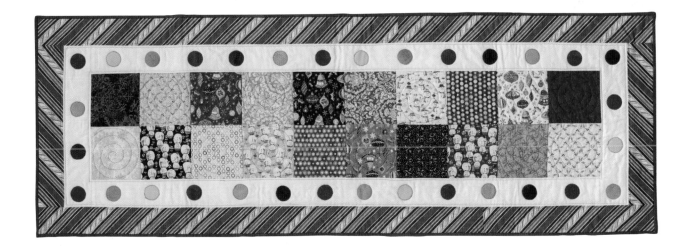

# Christmas Cracker Table Runner

The tradition of Christmas crackers dates back to nineteenth century England and is still popular today. A cracker is a brightly wrapped cardboard tube containing a paper crown, confetti, a riddle, a party favor or two, and a snapping device. When tablemates pull on opposite ends of a cracker, there's a loud snap and the cracker splits open, releasing its festive contents. Capture the excitement of the "pop," and the fun of flying confetti landing on the table, with this special Christmas runner.

**Designed and made by Mary Burns | Finished table runner: 23" x 50"**

## Materials

*Yardage is based on 42"-wide fabric.*

1½ yards of white-on-white print for background

¼ yard of green print for border

6 strips, 1½" x 42", of assorted dark Christmas prints for crackers

4 strips, 1½" x 42", of assorted light Christmas prints for crackers

Scraps (4" x 6" *each*) of red, green, gold, and turquoise felted wool for confetti

1 yard *each* of ½"-wide red, green, and gold rickrack

⅜ yard of red print for binding

1¾ yards of fabric for backing

29" x 56" piece of batting

6" x 24" and 6" x 6" acrylic rotary-cutting rulers with 45°-angle lines

See-through template plastic

Freezer paper (Optional)

Stapler and staples

## Cutting

**From the white-on-white print, cut:**

1 rectangle, 20½" x 47½"

**From the green print, cut:**

1 strip, 1¾" x 42"; crosscut into 2 strips, 1¾" x 20½"

3 strips, 1¾" x 42"

**From *each* color of felted wool, cut:**

12 squares, 1" x 1" (48 total)

16 squares, ½" x ½" (64 total)

**From *each* color of rickrack, cut:**

5 pieces, 6" long (15 total)

**From the red print, cut:**

4 strips, 2½" x 42"

## Strip Piecing and Cutting the Cracker Units

1. Lay out four dark and three light 1½"-wide strips in a pleasing order, alternating light and dark. Sew the strips together to make a strip set. Press the seam allowances toward the dark fabrics. Measure the strip set from raw edge to raw edge. It should measure 7½" wide. Make adjustments, if necessary.

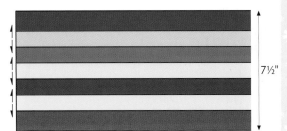

### Controlling the Bias

When working with diagonally cut units, you're sure to be handling bias-cut edges. To prevent stretching and distortion of these edges, press your strips with spray starch or starch alternative before sewing them together. The stiffer your strips are, the easier they will be to handle.

2. Starting 4" from the left edge of the strip set, place the 45°-angle line of a 6" x 24" rotary-cutting ruler along the first seam from the bottom as shown. Cut across the strip set along the right side of the ruler.

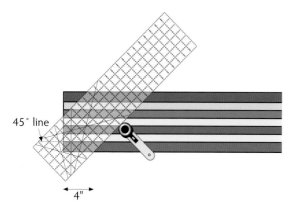

3. Keeping the 45°-angle line on the first seam, slide the ruler to the right so the 4½" line on the ruler is now aligned with the just-cut edge. Cut along the other side of the ruler to create a pieced section, 4½" wide.

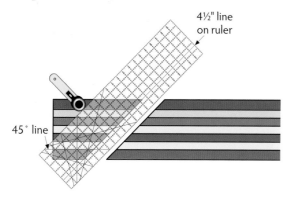

4. Reverse the ruler and slide it to the right so the 4½" line is on the just-cut edge and the 45°-angle line is again on the first seam. Cut along the right edge of the ruler. Repeat to cut three more 4½"-wide pieced sections for a total of five sections.

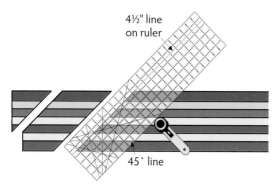

5. Align the 45°-angle line on a 6" square ruler with the third seam from the top of a section. Cut across the top and bottom of the ruler as shown to create a pieced rectangle and two pieced triangles. Repeat to yield five rectangles and seven triangles.

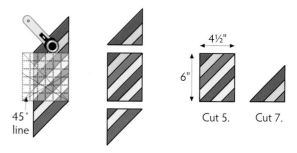

6. Sew together the remaining two dark and one light 1½" strips, alternating light and dark. Press the seam allowances toward the dark fabrics. Measure the strip set from raw edge to raw edge. It should measure 3½" wide. Make adjustments if necessary. Trace the triangle pattern (page 58), including the seam lines, onto see-through template plastic to make a template. Position the plastic template on the strip set, aligning the marked lines on the template with the seams of the strip set. Trace along the edges of the template and cut out on the marked lines. Repeat to cut a total of three pieced triangles.

## Appliquéing the Crackers

1. From the freezer paper, cut five rectangles, 3¾" x 5½". Center a rectangle on the wrong side of a pieced rectangle, shiny side up, matching two opposite corners to seams. Fold the

fabric over the freezer paper and press on all sides with a dry iron, folding the fabric under at the corners.

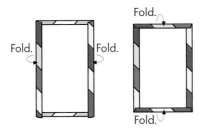

Fold 2 opposite sides,
then 2 remaining sides.

2. Cut five 3¾" squares from freezer paper. Cut the squares in half diagonally to yield 10 triangles. Center a triangle on the wrong side of pieced triangle, shiny side up. Fold the fabric over the freezer paper and press on all sides with a dry iron. To turn under the acute angles of the triangle, first fold the point over the freezer paper, and then fold the sides over one at a time to form a perfect point.

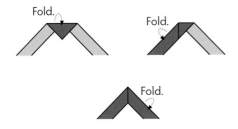

3. Referring to the photo (page 58) for placement, position the prepared rectangles and triangles on the white background rectangle, being sure not to place them within the ¼" seam allowance. Notice that the point of each triangle is centered on one end of a rectangle. If you wish to place your crackers symmetrically as Mary did, finger-press the background rectangle on both length and width to form creases to use as placement guides and use a ruler to measure equal distances from the edges for opposite crackers. You may prefer to place your crackers randomly. It's up to you!

4. Pin the rectangles and triangles in place. Appliqué the pieces to the background fabric by hand or machine. Mary used monofilament and a narrow machine zigzag stitch to stitch the appliqués in place. To remove the freezer paper, cut a small slit through the background fabric behind the appliqué and gently remove the freezer paper with your fingers or tweezers.

## Adding the Confetti

1. Place the appliquéd runner on a table and arrange the rickrack and wool confetti squares in a pleasing design, avoiding the ¼" seam allowance on all edges. Secure all in place with pins or staples.

### Confetti!

Mary tossed her rickrack pieces and wool squares up in the air and let them fall randomly on her appliquéd runner. She then moved them around just a bit until the colors and sizes looked balanced and she was happy with their placement.

2. Using white thread, hand or machine stitch the large wool squares in place with a starry snowflake design or any other motif you prefer.

3. Use monofilament and a small circle motif to stitch the small wool squares in place. Again using monofilament, secure the rickrack by folding under one of the ends and using a zigzag stitch to hold it in place. Use a machine straight stitch to sew through the center of the rickrack to the other end, and then fold under and secure that end with a zigzag stitch as before.

## Adding the Border

Sew the green 20½"-long strips to the ends of the table runner. Press the seam allowances toward the strips. Sew the remaining green strips end to end; from this strip, cut two 1¾" x 50" strips and sew them to the sides of the table runner. Press the seam allowances toward the strips.

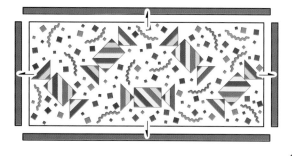

## Finishing the Table Runner

For help with any of the finishing steps, go to ShopMartingale.com/HowtoQuilt for free downloadable information.

1. Layer the table-runner top, batting, and backing; baste the layers together.

2. Hand or machine quilt as desired.

3. Using the red 2½"-wide strips, prepare and sew the binding to the table runner.

4. Add a label, if desired.

Pattern includes ¼" turn-under allowance on all sides.

*Seam line*

*Seam line*

**Triangle template**

# Diamond Mantel Cover

**B**ring a contemporary look to your holidays with this mantel cover. Fussy-cut motifs paired with embroidered stars add a touch of joy to any holiday room.

Designed and made by Cathy Valentine Reitan   |   Finished mantel cover: 18" x 40"

## Materials

*Yardage is based on 42"-wide fabric. Fat quarters measure 18" x 21".*

⅝ yard of red print for sashing and binding

¼ yard of gray-and-red print for diamonds

¼ yard of white wool for diamonds

¼ yard of gray-and-white print for triangles

1 fat quarter of red snowman print for fussy-cut diamonds*

¼ yard of white-and-red print for top panel

⅝ yard of fabric for backing

24" x 46" piece of batting

See-through template plastic

Size 12 variegated red pearl cotton

Transfer-Eze (optional)

8 small jingle bells

*You might need more or less than 1 fat quarter depending on the size of your fussy-cut motif and how often it's printed on the fabric.*

## Cutting

**From the red print, cut:**

1 strip, 1½" x 42"

8 strips, 1½" x 42"; crosscut into:

    17 strips, 1½" x 7"

    17 strips, 1½" x 8"

2 strips, 2¼" x 42"

**From the white-and-red print, cut:**

1 strip, 7" x 42"

## Making the Diamond Blocks

1. Using the pattern (page 62), trace the diamond shape five times onto the gray-and-red print and cut out on the drawn line. In the same manner, cut four white wool diamonds and five gray-and-white diamonds. Cut the gray-and-white diamonds in half horizontally to make 10 triangles. To fussy-cut the red snowman print, trace the pattern onto see-through template plastic and cut out. Center the template on a desired motif and trace around the edge of the template. Cut out the diamond on the drawn line.

2. Sew a red 7"-long strip to the top-left edge of a gray-and-red diamond, making sure that the strip extends at least 1½" beyond the top of the diamond. Press the seam allowances toward the strip. Trim the red strip even with the bottom edge of the diamond. Sew a red 8"-long strip to the top-right edge of the diamond, making sure that the strip extends beyond the other red strip. Trim the first red strip even with the second red strip. Press the seam allowances toward the red strip, and then trim the red strip even with the left edge of the diamond. Trim the red strip even with the bottom edge of the diamond to complete the block. Repeat to make a total of five gray-and-red blocks, four red snowman blocks, and eight white wool blocks.

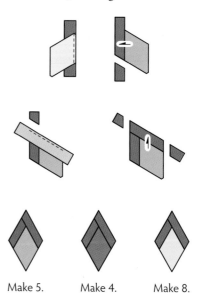

Make 5.     Make 4.     Make 8.

## Assembling the Mantel Cover

1. Sew two blocks together to make a row, adding a gray triangle to the top left corner of each. Make four rows each of the two combinations shown. In a similar manner, stitch two gray triangles to the top corners of the remaining gray-and-red diamond to make the right-edge unit of the mantel cover.

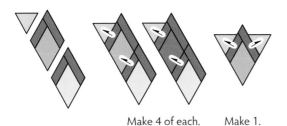

Make 4 of each.  Make 1.

2. Join the rows together as shown, aligning the seams of the red strips. Sew the right-edge unit to the right side of the joined rows, aligning the seams in the same manner. Place the ¾" line of your ruler even with the top point of the red or gray diamond in each row and trim across the top of the joined rows.

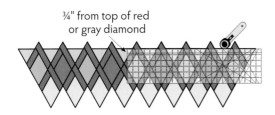

¾" from top of red or gray diamond

3. Sew the red 1½"-wide strip to the white-and-red 7" x 42" strip to make the top panel of the mantel cover. Press the seam allowances toward the red strip. Center the joined blocks on the edge of the panel and join.

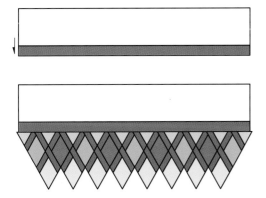

4. Position a ruler on the mantel cover so a horizontal line on the ruler is aligned with the top edge of the panel and the long edge of the ruler is positioned ¼" to the *outside* of the bottom point of the triangle on the far left. Trim the cover along the edge of the ruler. Repeat on the other end of the cover, trimming ¼" to the *outside* of the bottom point of the triangle on the far right.

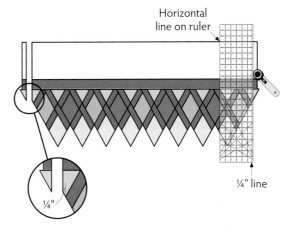

Horizontal line on ruler

¼" line

¼"

## Embroidering the Stars

1. Transfer the star design to the wool diamonds using your favorite transfer method. Cathy used Transfer Eze, a wash-away product that allows you to print your designs with your home printer/scanner, and then peel and stick the design to the diamonds.

2. Using the red pearl cotton, embroider the star motif in the center of each white diamond with a backstitch and French knots.

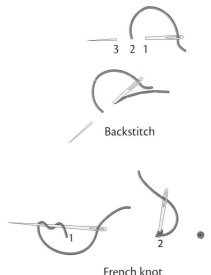

3  2  1

Backstitch

1  2

French knot

# Finishing the Quilt

For help with any of the finishing steps, go to ShopMartingale.com/HowtoQuilt for free downloadable information.

1. Layer the backing right side up on the batting. Place the top, right side down, on top of the backing. Smooth the layers and pin generously along the bottom (wool) edge only.

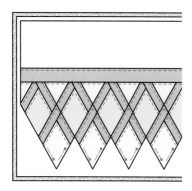

2. With a ¼" seam allowance, stitch along the bottom jagged edge of the mantel cover, starting at the wool diamond on the right. Do not stitch into the red on either outside edge. Trim the backing and batting even with the jagged bottom edge. Clip inside and outside points carefully.

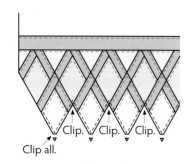

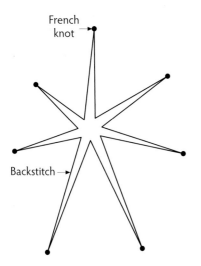

3. Turn right side out and carefully press the seam allowances toward the backing.

4. Quilt as desired. Cathy quilted only the red strips and the top panel.

5. Trim the quilt sandwich. Using the red 2¼"-wide strips, prepare the binding. Starting and ending the binding at the white diamonds, bind the sides and top of the cover.

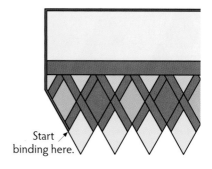

6. Sew jingle bells to the points of the white diamonds.

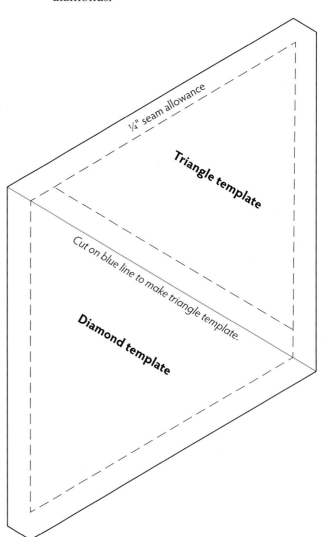

# Fireside Stars
# Mantel Cover

This mantel cover delivers lots of impact but is relatively quick and easy to assemble. English paper-pieced diamonds are arranged into stars and appliquéd to the background. The simple background, reminiscent of a star-studded midnight sky, is filled with gorgeous swirls of quilting.

| Designed and made by Mary V. Green; machine quilted by Krista Moser | Finished mantel cover: 20½" x 60" Finished blocks: 8" x 10¼" and 6" x 6⅞" |
| --- | --- |

## Materials

*Yardage is based on 42"-wide fabric. Fat quarters measure 18" x 21".*

2⅛ yards of blue fabric for background, backing, and binding

1 fat quarter *each* of 5 assorted yellow and gold fabrics for stars

22" x 62" piece of batting

45 paper diamonds for 6-pointed stars, 2" size (optional)*

Chalk marker or other light marker

*The diamond is measured along one side. A 6-pointed star is formed when 6 diamonds are sewn together.*

## Cutting

**From the *lengthwise* grain of the blue fabric, cut:**
2 rectangles, 21½" x 60½"

**From the *crosswise* grain of the blue fabric, cut:**
5 strips, 2¼" x 42"

**From *each* fat quarter, cut:**
2 strips, 2¼" x 20"; crosscut *each* into 5 pieces, 2¼" x 3½" (there will be 5 extra)

## Making the Stars

If you prefer to make your own paper templates rather than use purchased die-cut ones, trace the pattern (page 66) very carefully onto template plastic and cut it out. Trace around the template onto paper 45 times and cut out each piece. It's important to keep the tracing and cutting as accurate as possible so that the diamonds will fit together properly to form the stars.

1. Pin a paper diamond to the wrong side of 45 of the yellow 2¼" x 3½" pieces as shown. Trim the left and right sides of the fabric, leaving approximately ¼" seam allowance on all sides. Seam allowances do not have to be exact.

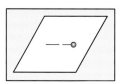

2. Turn the fabric to the back side of the template. Use a light-colored thread to baste the fabric to the paper, stitching through all layers. For the wide angles, make a small fold in the seam allowance to create a neat point. For the narrow, sharp angles, fold over and baste the outer points as shown, creating a sharp point.

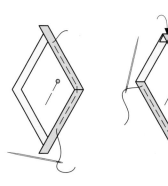

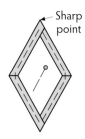

Sharp point

3. Arrange the basted diamonds into star shapes as shown.

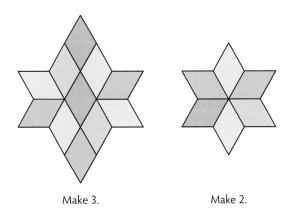

Make 3.          Make 2.

4. Whipstitch the edges together using matching thread.

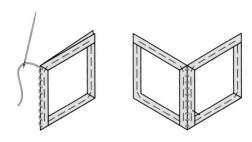

5. Press the stars well. Spray starch helps to keep the edges crisp. Remove the basting stitches and the paper pieces.

## Appliquéing the Stars

1. Finger-press one blue rectangle in half widthwise to form a vertical crease at the center. Place a large star on the crease, positioning it so that the bottom point is 1" above the bottom edge of the background. Place the other two large stars so that the bottom point is 1" from the bottom edge and 12" from the sides of the rectangle. Hand or machine appliqué the stars to the background.

2. Center the two smaller stars between the larger ones as shown, with the bottom point of the stars 6½" from the bottom edge of the background. Appliqué in place.

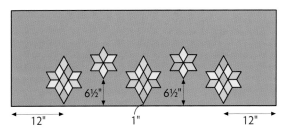

## Quilting and Finishing

1. The quilt was layered and quilted as a rectangle and then trimmed before binding. To accurately plan your quilting design, mark a line ½" outside the lower points of the large stars. Continue the line between the stars and to the outside edges of the rectangle.

2. Layer the backing, batting, and quilt top; baste. Outline quilt inside each diamond, and then fill the background with stitching, keeping the design inside the marked line.

3. Use a rotary cutter and ruler to carefully trim along the marked line.

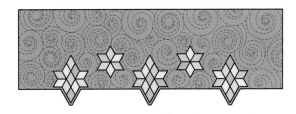

4. Using the blue strips, prepare and sew the binding to the quilt. The inner angles and the outer tips of the stars are mitered in the same way as a square quilt corner. Stitch to within ¼" of the first angle and backstitch. Fold the binding strip up so that it lines up with the second edge and creates a tuck, and then fold it down so that it is aligned with the second edge, and continue stitching. Note that these angles require a little more fabric than a typical right-angle miter. You may want to experiment a bit to get a feel for how they work.

5. Working on the front of the quilt, carefully press the binding away from the quilt center. This will make it easier to fold the miters. Fold and stitch the binding to the back of the quilt.

## Stitch It and Flip It

If you prefer to skip the binding, you can stitch the edges together before quilting. Mark and trim the lower edge as described above. Layer the backing rectangle *right side up* on the batting. Place the trimmed quilt top, *right side down*, on top of the backing rectangle. Smooth the layers and baste with pins. Using a ¼" seam allowance, stitch around the quilt top through all the layers, leaving a 10" opening along the top edge for turning. Trim away the excess batting and backing, leaving a ¼" seam allowance all the way around. Trim an additional ⅛" of batting around the star points. Turn the quilt right side out through the opening. Push the points out with a turning tool, being careful not to poke through the seam. Stitch the opening closed. Machine stitch around the outer edge of the quilt, ¼" from the edge, to create the appearance of a binding. Add additional quilting as desired.

## Make a Coordinating Table Runner

Instead of stitching around the star points and trimming the excess, leave the background fabric in a rectangle shape. Add a few more stars, quilt as desired, and finish with a traditional binding for a beautiful, matching table runner.

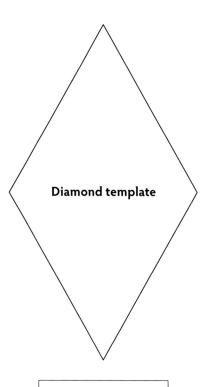

**Diamond template**

Pattern does not include seam allowances.

# Naturally Neutral Stocking

Santa wouldn't dare leave coal in a stocking that's so thoughtfully crafted from sweaters found at your local thrift shop—would he? Turn recycled wool sweaters and buttons into a stocking that add lots of warmth and texture to your mantel decor.

Designed and made by Karen Costello Soltys | Finished stocking: 8" x 21"

## Materials

3 or 4 sweaters, each with at least 80% wool content, in various shades of cream

½ yard of cotton Christmas print for stocking and cuff linings

1 yard of 17"-wide nonwoven stabilizer

Size 8 cream pearl cotton, or desired colors

Approximately 20 off-white buttons in assorted styles and sizes

## Preparing the Fabric

1. If you're starting with newly purchased sweaters or ones right out of your closet, wash and dry them before cutting them apart. Wash the sweaters in hot water with a little bit of detergent to felt them. Then toss them into a warm or hot dryer, but take them out before they completely dry; that can set in any wrinkles or creases.

2. Cut the sweaters apart along their seam lines (sleeves and side seams if the sweaters have them) and discard any ribbing or bands you don't want to use. If needed, lightly press the remaining pieces to remove wrinkles, but try not to flatten any design elements such as cables, ribs, or textured stitches.

### Save Time—Order Online!

Karen set out to support her local thrift stores, but found it hard to find sufficient off-white wool sweaters. If you're having a hard time finding what you need, check online at places like Etsy or eBay to see what some crafty vendor has already found at *her* local thrift shop. As Karen discovered, the price was right and much of the fabric prep work was already done.

## Piecing the Stocking

1. Using the patterns (pages 71–74), trace the four pattern parts onto one large piece of freezer paper or stabilizer to make a full-sized pattern. Use this pattern as a guide to make sure your patchwork sweater fabric will be large enough to cut out a complete shape.

2. Look over your assorted felted pieces of sweater and make a plan. Decide which pieces fit together best to make the most of your sweater fabric. Working with the first two pieces, cut a straight edge along each piece. Butt the two straight edges together on top of the stabilizer stocking and sew the edges together through all layers using a zigzag stitch and cream thread.

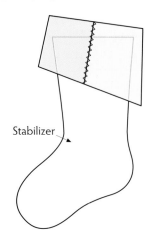

Stabilizer

Butt 2 sweater pieces together
on top of stabilizer
and zigzag stitch to join.

3. Remove the fabrics from the machine and decide which fabric to add next, and where. Fold the stabilizer back out of the way (it's okay to tear out the stitches that went through it), and using a rotary cutter and ruler, straighten the edge of the patchwork. Cut a straight edge along the piece you want to add. As before, butt

the two raw edges together (not overlapped) and zigzag the edges together. Continue in this manner until you've created a piece of fabric large enough to cover the stabilizer stocking pattern.

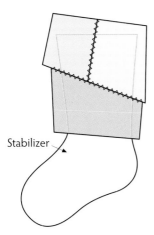

Stabilizer

Continue adding sweater pieces
to cover stabilizer stocking.

4. Using the stabilizer as a guide, cut out the stocking shape. If your stabilizer has shifted or crinkled, cut a fresh pattern from freezer paper and use it as a pattern to cut out the stocking.

5. Repeat steps 2–4 to create a second stocking piece for the back, flopping the stocking pattern to cut a mirror image.

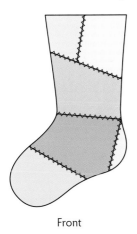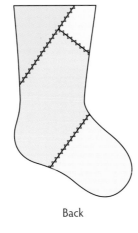

Front                    Back

6. Place the two stocking pieces right sides together and pin. Using a ½" seam allowance, sew the two pieces together, leaving the top edge open. If your sweater pieces are very thick, you may want to trim the seam allowances to reduce bulk. Press the seam allowances open as best as you can, and then turn the stocking right side out.

7. Pin the stocking pattern to the *folded* Christmas print and cut two pieces for the lining. Sew the lining pieces right sides together as you did for the stocking. Press, but do not turn.

8. Insert the lining inside the stocking, matching the side seams and top edge. Machine baste together along the top edge.

9. To make a hanging loop, cut a 1" x 6" piece of felted sweater. Fold it in half lengthwise and roll the long edges in toward fold. Pin, and then stitch along both long edges to secure. Fold the piece in half and baste across the raw edges to secure the loop.

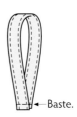

Baste.

10. To make the cuff, cut 4" x 16" strips of sweater fabric and cotton. Sew the short ends of each strip right sides together to make a ring; press the seam allowances open. With right sides together, sew the sweater and cotton rings together along one edge. Turn right side out and press.

**11.** With the cuff *inside* the stocking (and the sweater side toward the stocking lining), align the raw edges of the cuff with the raw edges of the stocking. Position the hanging loop at the side seam of the stocking, raw edges aligned and sandwiched between the stocking and the cuff. Using a ½"-wide seam allowance and stitching slowly because of the bulk, sew the cuff to the stocking. Use a walking foot if you have one for better control. Turn the cuff right side out and arrange the cuff as desired.

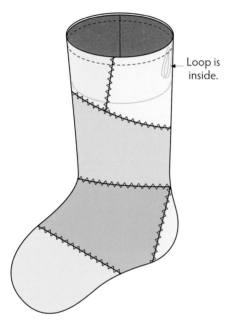

Loop is inside.

Stitch cuff to stocking.

# Embellishing the Stocking

**1.** To decorate the edges where the sweater pieces have been joined in a Crazy-quilt style, use the pearl cotton and an embroidery needle to stitch over the seam lines. Feather stitch, herringbone stitch, and cross-stitch all work well for this purpose.

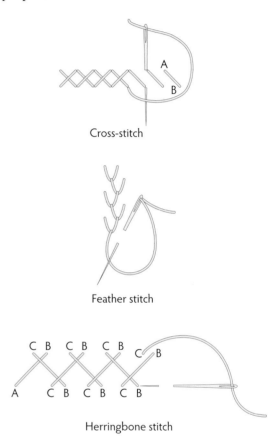

Cross-stitch

Feather stitch

Herringbone stitch

**2.** Sew buttons to the cuff, placing them randomly or in a pattern that pleases you. Don't forget to decorate all the way around!

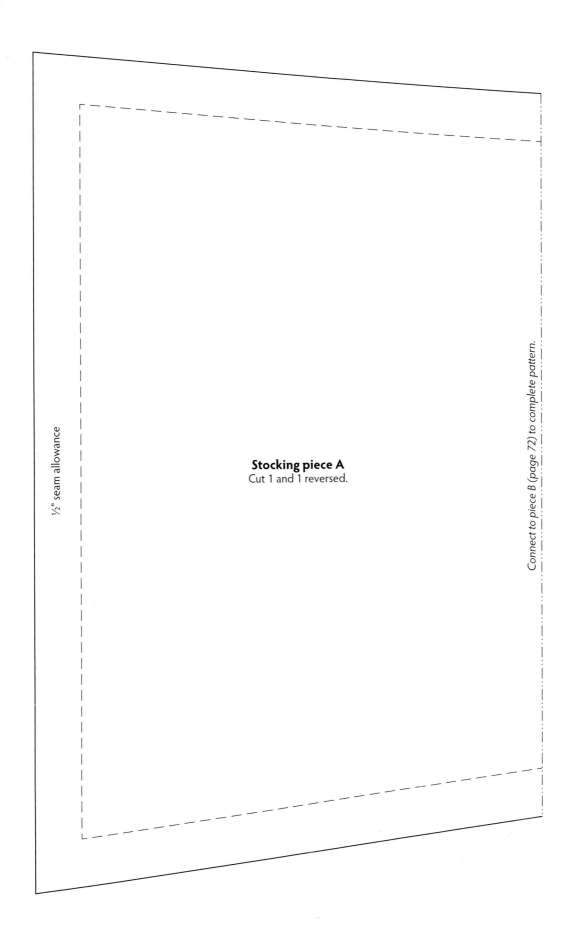

½" seam allowance

**Stocking piece A**
Cut 1 and 1 reversed.

Connect to piece B (page 72) to complete pattern.

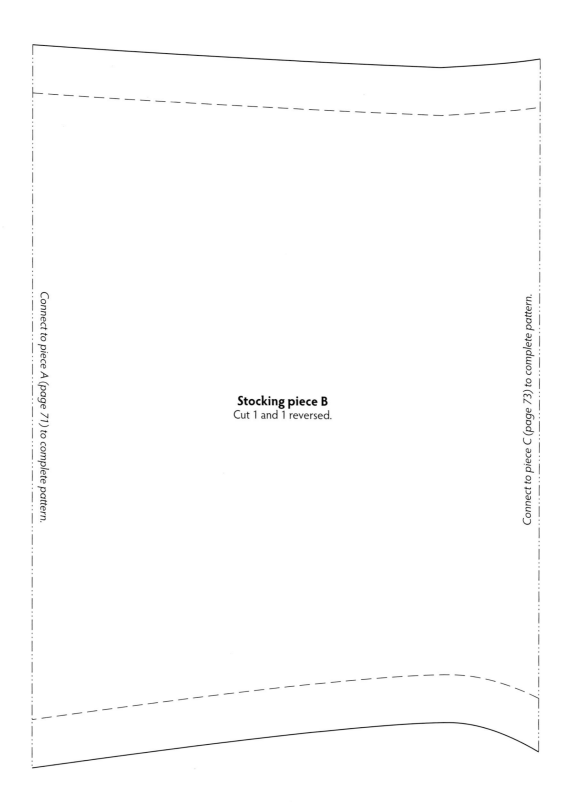

**Stocking piece B**
Cut 1 and 1 reversed.

Connect to piece A (page 71) to complete pattern.

Connect to piece C (page 73) to complete pattern.

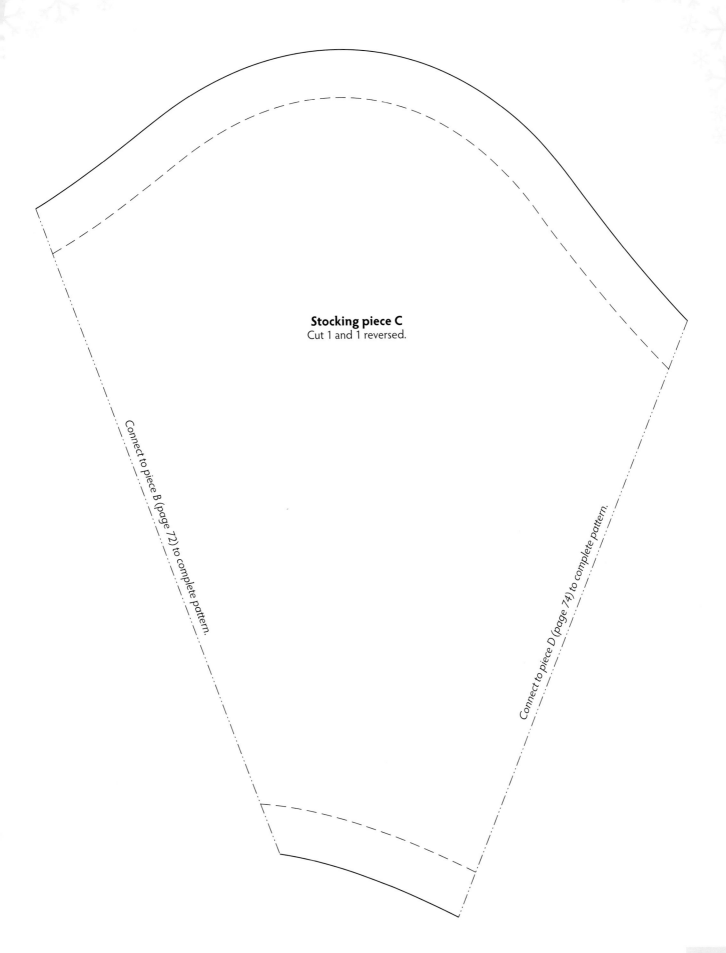

**Stocking piece C**
Cut 1 and 1 reversed.

Connect to piece B (page 72) to complete pattern.

Connect to piece D (page 74) to complete pattern.

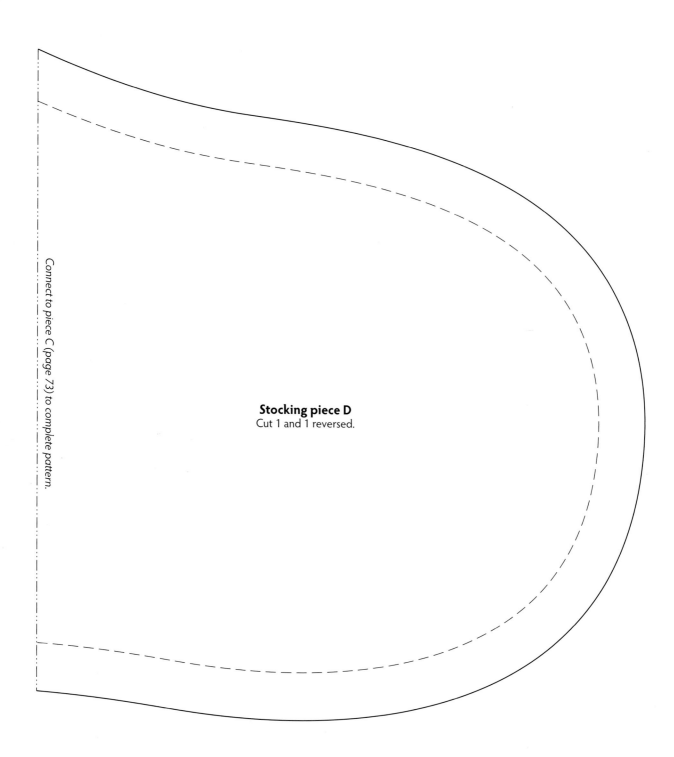

Connect to piece C (page 73) to complete pattern.

**Stocking piece D**
Cut 1 and 1 reversed.

# Pretty Party Purse

se some of the wonderful fabrics in your stash to make a slew of purses just right for gifts or for dressing up your favorite party dress. Whether you go for basic black or large floral prints, this project is sure to add charm to your wardrobe.

Designed and made by Cathy Valentine Reitan | Finished purse: Approximately 7" x 9½"

## Materials

*Yardage is based on 42"-wide fabric. Directions are for the black embroidered purse.*

½ yard of black satiny fabric for purse

½ yard of black cotton for lining

1 yard of 20"-wide black, woven fusible interfacing (such as Shape-Flex)

5" rounded purse frame

36" purse chain

Size 8 black, red, and green pearl cotton

1 sheet of Transfer-Eze

3 small sew-on gold crystals

## Cutting

**From the black cotton, cut:**

1 rectangle, 3¼" x 7"

**From the interfacing, cut:**

1 rectangle, 3¼" x 7"

## Adjusting and Cutting the Purse Pattern

Depending on the frame you're using, you may need to adjust the pattern so the purse body fits the frame properly.

1. Lay your purse frame on the purse pattern (page 79). Align the hinges on your frame with the dots on the pattern.

2. Draw around the top of your frame. This reshapes the template to fit your frame. You may need to adjust the sides of your template if your purse frame is significantly different from Cathy's. Cut the top edge of your adjusted template ½" outside your newly drawn line, easing the line of your new shape into the existing curve below the dots.

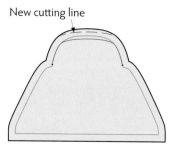

New cutting line

3. Using your template from step 2, cut out two purse shapes from the black satiny fabric, two from the black cotton, and four from the interfacing. Following the manufacturer's instructions, fuse the interfacing pieces to the wrong sides of the black purse shapes. Fuse the previously cut interfacing 3¼" x 7" rectangle to the cotton rectangle.

## Transferring the Embroidery Motif

1. With one of the satin purse shapes right side up, use your favorite method to transfer the poinsettia motif (page 80) to the lower-right corner of the shape, ½" from both the side and the bottom to allow for the ½" seam allowance. Cathy used a product called Tranfer-Eze,

available at quilt shops or online. There are other similar products available for easy marking.

2. Use the green pearl cotton to backstitch the leaves and the red pearl cotton to backstitch the flower petals. Sew gold crystals to the center of your poinsettia.

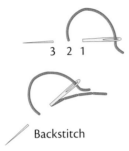

3   2   1

Backstitch

## Sewing the Purse

1. Backstitching at both ends of the seam, and with right sides together and edges aligned, sew the two black satin purse shapes together using a ½" seam allowance. Begin at one dot, sew around and across the bottom, and then end at the second dot.

2. Clip to the dots, being careful not to clip through your stitching. Clip the curves and trim the bottom corners diagonally.

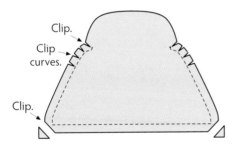

Clip.

Clip
curves.

Clip.

3. Press the seam allowances open using a sewing ham to support the underside of the seam. (A tennis ball works well if you don't have a sewing ham handy.) To box the corners, refold the purse (right sides together) so that a side seam matches up with the bottom seam, forming a triangle. Draw a line perpendicular to the bottom seam and ½" from the point of triangle. Stitch on this line forward, backward, and forward again for extra strength in the seam. Repeat to box the other corner. Turn the purse right side out and press.

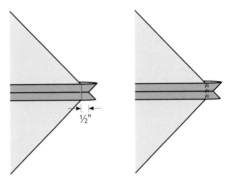

½"

## Sewing the Lining

1. To make an inside pocket for your driver's license or credit card, fold the prepared rectangle in half widthwise with right sides together. Leaving a 2" opening on one side for turning, use a ¼" seam to stitch around the three unfolded sides. Clip all four corners diagonally to reduce bulk. Turn right side out and push out the corners with a dull pencil or knitting needle, being careful not to poke through the seam. Run the tool along the seam all the way around to help flatten the edges of the pocket. Hand stitch the opening closed.

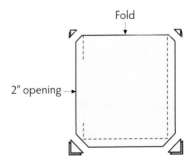

Fold

2" opening

2. Finger-press one purse lining piece in half vertically and the pocket in half lengthwise to find the centers. Matching the center creases, position the pocket on the right side of the purse lining with the folded edge of the pocket 2" down from the top edge of the lining. Topstitch ⅛" from the sides and bottom of the pocket to secure it.

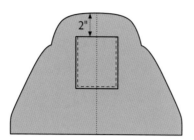

3. Repeat steps 1–3 of "Sewing the Purse," but don't turn your lining right side out. Insert the lining into the purse, *wrong* sides together. Align the side seams of the purse and the lining at the top edge of the purse.

4. Pin the lining and the purse together around the top edges and stay stitch ¼" from the edges all the way around. Press the edges inward along the stitching line, toward the lining.

## Attaching the Frame

Frames come in both sew-on and glue-in models. The process for positioning the frame is the same for both. Cathy used a sew-on frame. Follow the manufacturer's directions for attaching the purse to your frame if they differ from the following instructions.

1. Position the frame by lining up the side hinges with the side seams and the center front and back at the top of the purse with the center points at the top of the frame. Use curved safety pins or clothespins to hold the purse to the frame.

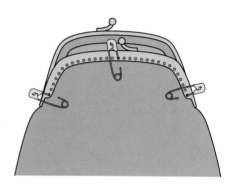

2. Push the pressed-over edge at the top of the purse into the frame and use the black pearl cotton to stitch the frame to the purse body. If you have a glue-in frame, squeeze a narrow bead of fabric or craft glue into the groove of the frame prior to pushing the pressed edge of the purse into the frame. Use a stiletto to push the fabric securely into the glued groove and follow the manufacturer's directions for drying time.

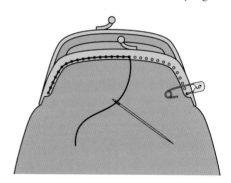

3. Attach the chain to the purse frame and enjoy the party!

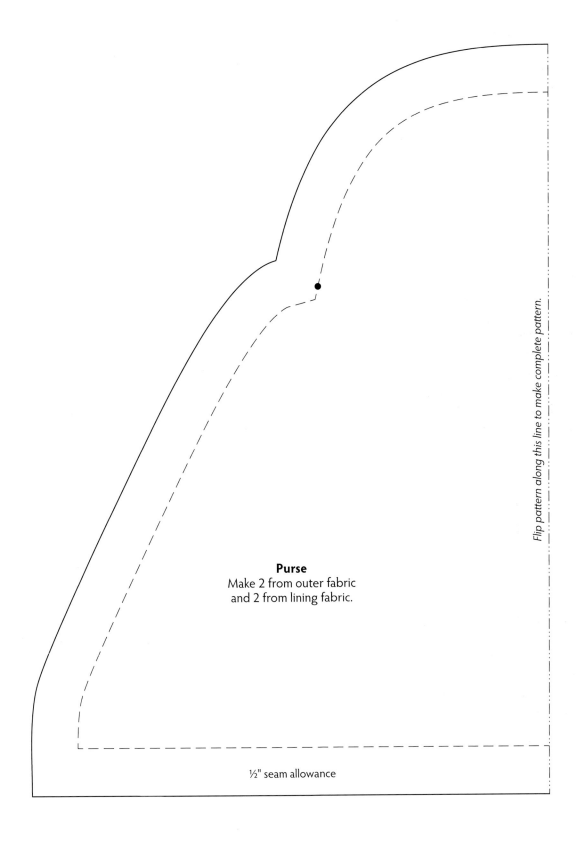

**Purse**
Make 2 from outer fabric
and 2 from lining fabric.

½" seam allowance

Flip pattern along this line to make complete pattern.

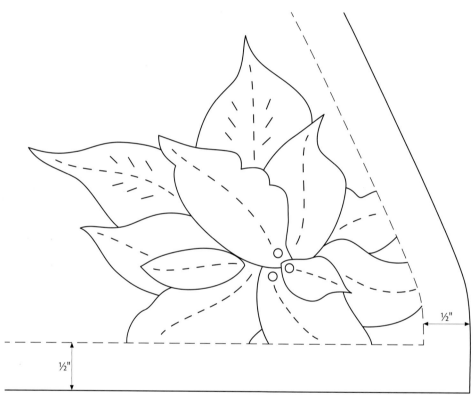

**Embroidery placement**

# Snowflake Pillows

This trio of snowflake pillows features contrasting textures of felted wool and silk dupioni. Add a bit of "bling" with glass beads if you wish. The snowflakes are easy to appliqué and fun to create. Use the patterns provided, or cut your own designs—just like when you were in grade school!

| Designed and made by Karen Costello Soltys | Finished pillows: 12" x 12" (red and green); 11" x 16" (blue) |
| --- | --- |

## Materials

*Materials are sufficient for all 3 pillows.*

½ yard of 44"-wide silk dupioni for *each* pillow (red, blue, and green)

½ yard of 50"-wide off-white felted wool for appliqués

1½ yards of 17"-wide nonwoven fusible interfacing

9" zippers in colors to match silk (1 per pillow)

Size 6 clear glass beads, about 50 per pillow (optional)

Pillow forms or polyester fiberfill (Karen used 12" square pillow forms for the square pillows and fiberfill for the rectangular pillow)

Cotton thread to match wool for appliqué (such as YLI or Coats)

Freezer paper

## Preparing the Fabric

1. Using a dry iron on the silk setting, press the silk fabrics to remove any creases. For the square pillows, cut a 14" square of fabric and fuse a 13½" square of interfacing to the wrong side, following the manufacturer's instructions and taking care not to scorch the silk. Trim the square to 13" x 13". For the rectangular pillow, repeat the process, starting with a 13" x 18" piece of silk and a 12½" x 17½" piece of interfacing. *Note:* The interfacing will give the silk body to support the appliqué, and also help keep the silk from fraying as you handle it during appliqué.

2. To make the snowflakes, cut a 10" square of freezer paper for the larger snowflakes and an 8" square of freezer paper for the smaller one. With the dull side out, fold the papers in half diagonally, and then diagonally again. Fold the

triangular shape into thirds as shown. Fold as carefully as possible for a symmetrical snowflake, and then crease the folds sharply.

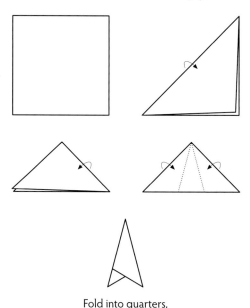

Fold into quarters,
then into thirds.

3. Trace the patterns (pages 85 and 86) or your own design onto the prepared freezer-paper wedges and cut out along the lines. Open the freezer paper to reveal your snowflakes. If you want to make adjustments, refold along the crease lines and make any additional cuts you'd like.

4. With your iron on the wool setting, press the freezer-paper templates onto the right side of the wool and cut out exactly on the drawn lines. You may find it easier to mark any interior lines with a pencil or marking pen since the freezer paper won't adhere to the wool as firmly as it does to cotton fabric.

5. Also trace the letters S, N, and W (pages 85 and 86) onto the dull side of the freezer paper and cut out on the drawn lines. Iron the templates onto the right side of the wool and cut out.

## Appliquéing the Pillows

1. For the square pillows, fold the prepared silk squares in half vertically and horizontally and finger-press to mark positioning lines. Using the lines as guides, center a large wool snowflake on each square and pin or baste in place.

Use creases as guides
for positioning snowflake.

2. Using white cotton thread and a hand-sewing needle, stitch the snowflake in place using an overcast stitch. Pull the thread snugly, but not too tight, and it will become lost in the loft of the wool for a nearly invisible appliqué stitch. Stitch into the wool about 1/16". Karen stitched around the perimeter first, and then along all interior cutouts.

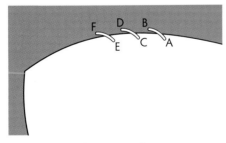

Overcast stitch.
Come up at A, C, and E,
and down at B, D, and F.

3. For the rectangular pillow, place the letters and the snowflake so they spell out the word *snow*. Notice that the pieces are not all aligned horizontally; you can place them at any jaunty angle you like. Because the wool is very flexible and forgiving, you can bend the letters into slightly different positions than what's shown. When you're satisfied with the arrangement, pin the letters in place and stitch them to the silk background.

## Assembling the Pillows

1. Trim the square pillows to 12½" x 12½", centering the appliqué. Trim the rectangular pillow to 11½" x 16½", making sure to leave at least 1" outside of all appliqués for seam allowance.

2. To make the pillow backs, fuse interfacing to the wrong side of the remaining silk and cut the following pieces: For each square pillow, cut two rectangles, 8" x 13". For the rectangular pillow, cut two pieces, 10" x 12". Align the longer edges of two backing rectangles, right sides together. Using a 5/8"-wide seam allowance, stitch 1½" along the 13" edges; then backstitch. Set the stitch length on your machine for a long basting stitch and sew for 9". Reset the stitch length to the regular length and continue sewing to the end of the seam. Press the seam allowances open.

1½"

9"

## Silk Secrets

* Regular sewing pins can leave holes in your silk. A box of silk pins is inexpensive and will last for years.

* Never use steam when ironing silk. One drop of water can leave a permanent mark.

* Don't forget to use the silk setting on your iron. It takes just seconds to scorch your lovely silk.

* If possible, pin silk parallel to the seam and only within the seam allowance.

* Always use a brand-new needle when sewing with silk, and if you find that your fingertips are snagging the silk, use a nail file or emery board to gently file your fingernails and use hand lotion to smooth out roughness on your skin.

3. Insert a lapped zipper (a *lapped zipper* is one in which the fold of the fabric covers the teeth of the zipper) into the pillow back as follows: Switch the presser foot to the zipper foot. Position the zipper right side down on the seam allowance. Pin one side of the zipper tape to the seam allowance only, along the portion that has been basted. The zipper teeth should be just to the side of the seam, not directly on top of it. Fold the pillow backing out of the way and stitch the zipper tape to the seam allowance only. Fold the seam allowance back so that you form a pleat of fabric alongside the zipper tape you just stitched. The fold should not quite touch the zipper teeth. Using a regular stitch length, stitch between the fold and the seam.

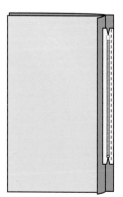

Stitch close to fold.

4. Turn the pillow back right side up and press along the basted seam line to smooth. Starting at the bottom of the zipper teeth, topstitch across the bottom of the zipper through all layers. Pivot and continue stitching along the side of the zipper that has not already been stitched. Pivot again and stitch across the top of the zipper teeth, taking care not to stitch into the metal zipper stop. Using your seam ripper, carefully remove the basting stitches.

Topstitch along top,
bottom and side of zipper.

5. Trim the completed pillow back to 12½" square for the square pillows and 11½" x 16½" for the rectangular pillow.

6. Open the zipper and place the pillow back right sides together with the matching pillow top. Pin and the stitch around all edges using a ¼" seam allowance. Press the seam allowances open or to one side and trim the corners diagonally. Turn the pillow right side out; press using a warm iron and a pressing cloth.

## Finishing the Pillows

1. If desired, use beads to add some glitz to the wool appliqués. Thread a sewing needle with a long length of thread, bring the ends together, and tie a knot. Bring the needle up from the wrong side, slip it through the bead, and back down through the pillow top. Sew through each bead three or four times, and then move on to the next bead. Fasten off and start a new thread when needed.

2. Insert the pillow form or stuffing into each pillow and zip it closed.

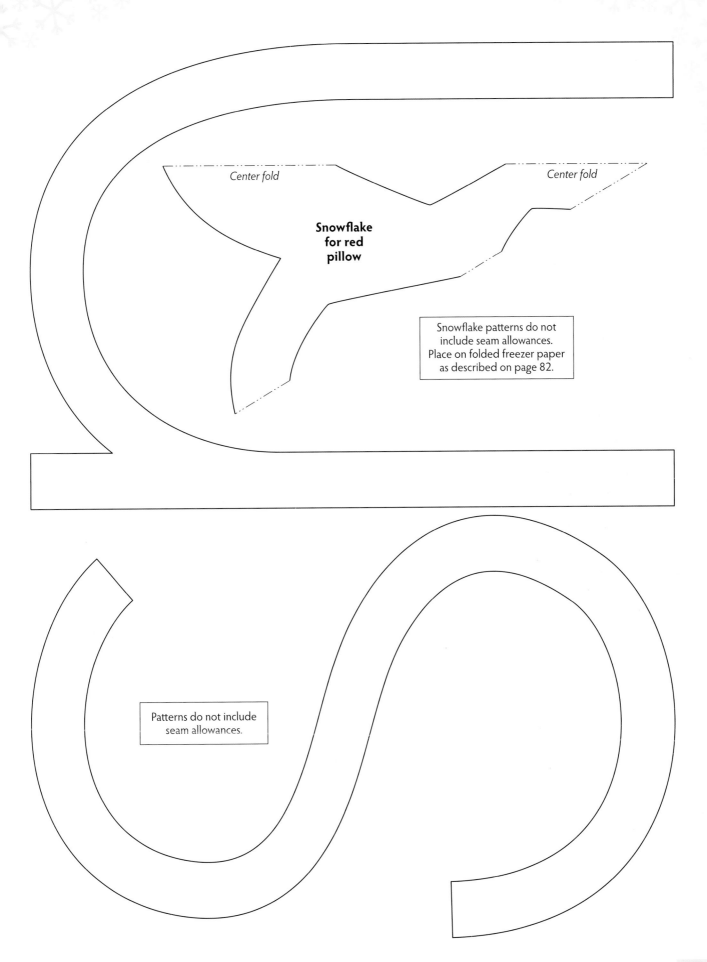

Center fold

Center fold

**Snowflake
for red
pillow**

Snowflake patterns do not
include seam allowances.
Place on folded freezer paper
as described on page 82.

Patterns do not include
seam allowances.

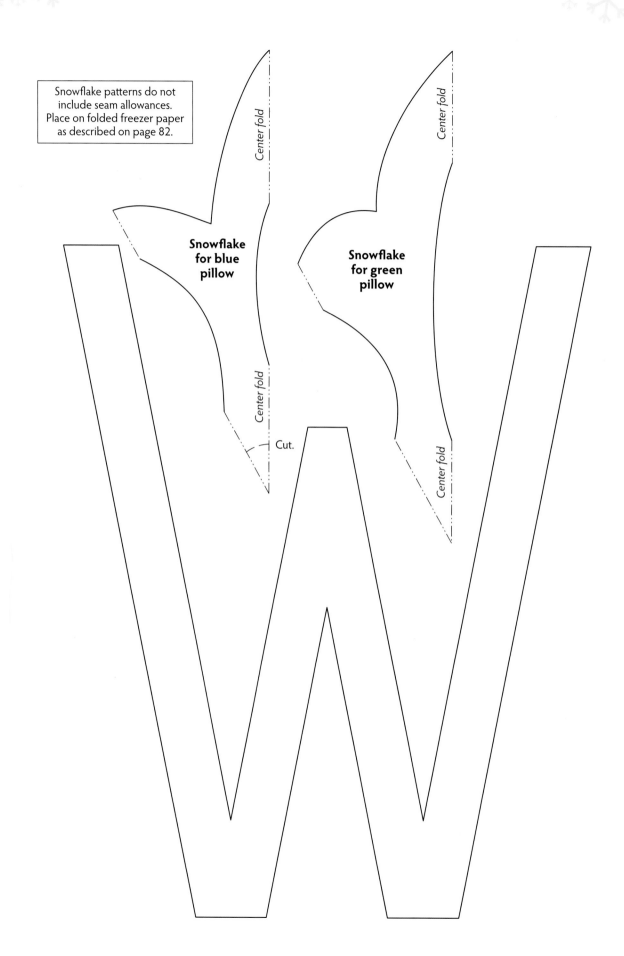

Snowflake patterns do not include seam allowances. Place on folded freezer paper as described on page 82.

*Center fold*

*Center fold*

**Snowflake for blue pillow**

**Snowflake for green pillow**

*Center fold*

*Center fold*

Cut.

# Christmas Cookie Apron

**M**ary's quilt group held a tea-towel challenge, and this fat-quarter-friendly ruffled apron made with Christmas prints was her response. You can baste and gather the ruffles the old-fashioned way, or use a ruffling foot if you have one for your machine for even faster results. Make one for all your friends and have a stylish Christmas cookie baking party!

Designed and made by Mary Burns | Finished apron: 17¾" x 27"

## Materials

*Yardage is based on 42"-wide fabric. Fat quarters measure 18" x 21".*

1 fat quarter of light-green print for tie

1 fat quarter of dark-green print for ruffle

1 fat quarter of gold print for ruffle

1 fat quarter of multicolored stripe for ruffle

1 fat quarter of multicolored print for ruffle

1 purchased red tea towel, 18" x 27", for base of apron*

1 yard of 1½"-wide turquoise rickrack for trim

Bodkin or safety pin for turning tubes

*\*Size of tea towel doesn't have to be exact.*

## Cutting

**From the multicolored stripe, cut:**
3 strips, 5½" x 20"

**From the gold print, cut:**
3 strips, 5½" x 20"

**From the dark-green print, cut:**
3 strips, 5½" x 20"

**From the multicolored print, cut:**
3 strips, 5½" x 20"

**From the light-green print, cut:**
4 strips, 2¾" x 20"

## Making and Attaching the Ruffles

1. Sew the striped strips end to end to make one 5½" x 59" strip; press the seam allowances open. In the same manner, make gold, dark green, and multicolored 5½" x 59" strips; press the seam allowances open.

2. Fold ½" under on both short ends of the striped strip and press. Fold the strip in half lengthwise, right sides together, and press. Using matching thread, topstitch ¼" from each short end to form a hem. Trim the stitched corners diagonally and turn the strip right side out; press. Repeat with the remaining 59"-long strips.

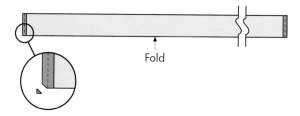

Fold

3. Fold the striped strip in half to find the center and make a small mark on the raw edge using a pencil or pen. Machine baste ⅛" and ¼" from the raw edges of the strip. Gather the strip along the basting threads until it is about 27" long, or the length of your tea towel. Repeat with the remaining 59"-long strips.

4. With a pencil and ruler, measure and mark a line 1" from a long edge of the tea towel. (This edge will become the bottom edge of the apron.) Mark another line 1¾" above, and parallel to, the first. Repeat twice to mark a total of

four lines. Fold the tea towel in half and make a small mark at the center of each drawn line.

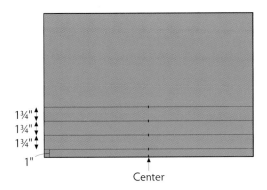

1¾"
1¾"
1¾"
1"

Center

5. Matching center marks and arranging the gathers evenly, align and pin the raw edge of the striped ruffle to the lowest marked line on the towel. Stitching ¼" from the raw edge of the ruffle, sew the ruffle to the towel. In the same manner, stitch the gold ruffle along the second line, the dark-green ruffle along the third line, and the multicolored ruffle along the top line.

## Making the Casing and Tie

1. To form the casing for the tie, fold 2" to the wrong side of the tea towel along the top edge. Press; then pin in place. Using red thread, topstitch ⅛" from the folded edge of the towel, 1⅞" from the fold, and again 1¾" from the fold to form the tie casing.

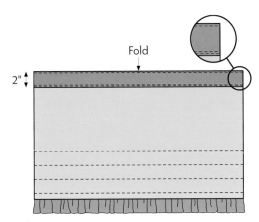

Fold

2"

2. Sew the light-green strips end to end to make one 2¾" x 78½" strip; press the seam allowances open. At each end of the strip, fold in the corners, wrong sides together, to meet in the center. Press.

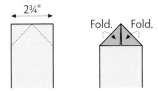

2¾"

Fold. Fold.

3. Fold the strip in half lengthwise, right sides together. Sew using a ¼" seam allowance along the long raw edge. Using a bodkin or a safety pin on the end of shoelace, turn the tube right side out. Roll the tube between your fingers to flatten the seam allowances within; press. Using matching thread, topstitch the mitered ends in place ⅛" from the edge.

⅛"

## Finishing the Apron

1. Cut a 30" length of rickrack. Turn under ½" on each end and topstitch ⅛" from the fold using matching thread. Mark the center of the rickrack with a pin. Matching the centers, place the rickrack on the top edge of the multicolored ruffle, hiding the raw edges of the ruffle and extending 1" over the left and right edges of the apron. Pin in place. Fold the ends to the back of tea towel. Pin. Check to make sure that the raw edge of the ruffle is completely hidden under the rickrack.

2. Using matching thread, sew along one long edge of the rickrack, pivot, and then sew across the end of the rickrack, catching the rickrack end on the back of the towel in the stitching. Pivot again, sew back along the other long edge of the rickrack, pivot, and then stitch across the other end of the rickrack in the same manner.

3. Use a bodkin or safety pin to slide the light green tie through the casing. Wrap it around your waist, tie a bow, and start baking cookies!

# Forest Friends
# Holiday Ornaments

Dress up your tree with this cast of charming and festive woodland characters. These easy, hand-stitched projects would also make great stocking stuffers and are the perfect addition to a creatively wrapped gift.

Designed and sewn by Adrienne Smitke | Finished ornaments: Approximately 2" wide to 4¼" tall

## Materials

2 sheets, 12" x 18", of white felt for ornament foundations and toadstool spots

8" x 8" piece of felt in each of the following colors: bright red, medium red, green, medium green, tan, dark brown, medium gray, dark gray, and teal

Small scrap of medium-brown felt for bear's muzzle

Small scrap of light-gray felt for raccoon's muzzle

6-strand embroidery floss and sewing threads in assorted colors*

Permanent fabric glue

1 yard of 2 mm silver cord for hanging loops

Small hole punch for cutting out berries, hedgehog nose, and Christmas garland (optional)

Freezer paper for transferring patterns to felt (optional)

Water-soluble stabilizer for transferring embroidery patterns (optional)

*Refer to photo (page 90) and pattern pieces (page 95) for embroidery floss and thread colors.*

## Assembling the Ornaments

Read "Getting Started with Felt!," right, to learn Adrienne's techniques for tracing shapes and transferring embroidery patterns. Using the patterns (page 95), cut out two white foundation shapes for each ornament and set them aside. Cut out the remaining pattern shapes for each ornament. Refer to the embroidery-stitch diagrams (page 94) as needed and follow the instructions below to assemble each ornament. All embroidery is done with threads that match the felt color, except where noted.

### Getting Started with Felt!

If you've never worked with felt before, you're in for a treat! Here are a few of Adrienne's favorite tips to start you off:

* Not all felt is the same. Adrienne prefers a craft felt that's a blend of rayon and wool. It's soft, yet still yields clean edges when cutting out detailed shapes. You can also use polyester craft felt, 100% wool felt, or mix and match all three.

* To transfer patterns, use a fine-point permanent marker to trace pattern pieces onto the dull side of a piece of freezer paper. Roughly cut out the shapes, leaving ¼" around the lines, and then use a dry iron to adhere them to the felt. Cut out the felt shape on the traced lines and remove the remaining freezer paper.

* Sharp scissors with small, pointy tips are the key to cutting accurate shapes from felt.

* Use a small-diameter hole punch to cut out the holly berries, hedgehog nose, and Christmas tree garland. If you don't have a hole punch, you can also use small confetti-sized scraps of felt for these pieces.

* Use permanent, clear-drying fabric glue (such as Liquid Stitch) to tack some of the pieces together. It's important to use this glue sparingly since it dries hard and become difficult to sew or embroider through.

* Most of the embroidery designs on these ornaments are easy enough to stitch freehand. However, if you wish to transfer embroidery patterns directly to the felt ornament, trace the pattern onto a scrap of water-soluble stabilizer. Pin the stabilizer to the ornament and stitch through the layers. When finished, spray the stabilizer with water or use a soft damp cloth to dissolve the stabilizer.

## Embroidery Tips

Adrienne uses both embroidery floss and sewing thread on her ornaments, depending on the look she wants. Embroidery floss is made up of six strands; she often uses three strands to embroider, creating a bolder effect than when stitching with standard-weight sewing thread. To achieve a look closer to sewing thread, use just one or two strands of floss. For an even thicker line, use four, five, or six strands. Experiment with mixing and matching different thread and floss weights to create a variety of effects on your ornaments.

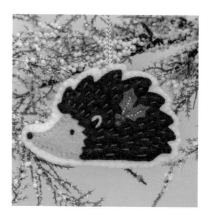

## Festive Hedgehog

1. Use fabric glue to tack the hedgehog body to the edge of the hedgehog face. Tack the ear, holly leaves, and holly berries to the hedgehog body.

2. Use small stipple stitches to cover the hedgehog body with spines. Stitch the outline of the hedgehog's eye and inner ear; fill in both with satin stitches.

3. Use light-green thread to backstitch through the middle of each holly leaf. Make a small French knot in the center of each holly berry to secure in place.

4. Using fabric glue, tack the hedgehog to a white-felt foundation piece. Tack the hedgehog's nose to his face. Secure the nose in place with a small French knot. Blanket-stitch around the entire perimeter of the hedgehog, stitching it to the foundation piece. Change colors as needed.

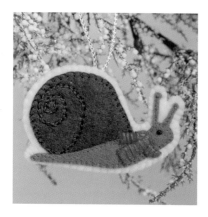

## Chilly Snail

1. Use fabric glue to tack the snail body in place along the bottom edge of the snail shell. Blanket-stitch the edge of the snail body to secure it in place.

2. Backstitch the swirl design to the snail shell using gray and teal floss. Use teal floss to make a small French knot for the snail's eye.

3. Use fabric glue to tack the scarf pieces to the snail body. Embroider the stripes and fringe of the scarf, catching the edges of the scarf to help secure it to the snail.

4. Using fabric glue, tack the snail to a white-felt foundation piece. Blanket-stitch around the entire perimeter of the snail body and shell, stitching the snail to the foundation piece. Change colors as needed. Use a small running stitch to stitch through the middle of the snail antennae, ending with a French knot, to secure them in place.

## Itchy Holiday Sweater Bear

1. Use fabric glue to tack down the tree trunk and tree to the bear's sweater. Tack the sweater and muzzle to the bear.

2. Use a short running stitch to embroider along the edge of the sweater's neck, sleeves, and hem. Use a stem stitch to embroider lines between the sweater arms and body.

3. Stitch around the perimeter of the tree trunk. Use small stipple stitches to cover the tree with pine needles.

4. Embroider the bear's mouth, and then stitch the outline of the bear's nose and eyes. Fill them in with satin stitch.

5. Using fabric glue, tack the bear to a white-felt foundation piece. Blanket-stitch around the entire perimeter of the bear, stitching it to the foundation piece. Change colors as needed.

## Woodland Christmas Tree

1. Use fabric glue to tack the felt ornaments to the tree. Use a small running stitch and white floss to embroider the garland, catching each of the ornaments with at least one stitch. Using pink and white floss, add French knots to fill out the garland.

2. Use green floss and small stipple stitches to fill in the areas of the tree between the garlands with pine needles.

3. Using fabric glue, tack the tree to a white-felt foundation piece. Blanket-stitch around the entire perimeter of the tree, stitching it to the foundation piece.

## Fancy Holiday Sweater Raccoon

1. Use fabric glue to tack the sweater, mask, and muzzle on the raccoon body.

2. Use a short running stitch and pink thread to embroider along the neck and hem of the sweater. Use a snowflake stitch to add small stars randomly across the sweater body.

3. Embroider the raccoon's mouth. Stitch the outline of the raccoon's nose and eyes, and then fill in with satin stitch. Use a short running stitch to stitch around the edge of the raccoon's mask.

4. Using fabric glue, tack the raccoon body to a white-felt foundation piece. Tack the tail on top of the raccoon body, and then tack the stripes to the tail. Use a short running stitch to stitch along the edges of the tail stripes.

5. Blanket-stitch around the entire perimeter of the raccoon, stitching it to the foundation piece. Change colors as needed.

## Toadstool

1. Use fabric glue to tack the white spots and the cap underside to the toadstool cap. Blanket-stitch the spots to the cap to secure in place.

2. Use fabric glue to tack the toadstool cap to a white-felt foundation piece. Tack the stem to the toadstool cap and the foundation piece. Backstitch the gills on the cap underside.

**3.** Blanket-stitch around the edges of the toadstool cap, cap underside, and stem, stitching the toadstool to the foundation piece. Change colors as needed.

## Finishing the Ornaments

Cut the silver cord into six pieces, each approximately 6" long. Fold a piece of cord in half and stitch the ends to the back of the white foundation of an ornament to secure in place. Using fabric glue, tack the remaining corresponding white-felt foundation piece on the back of the first, sandwiching the cord ends between the two layers. To finish, use white floss to blanket-stitch the two foundation layers together around the edges. Repeat with the remaining ornaments.

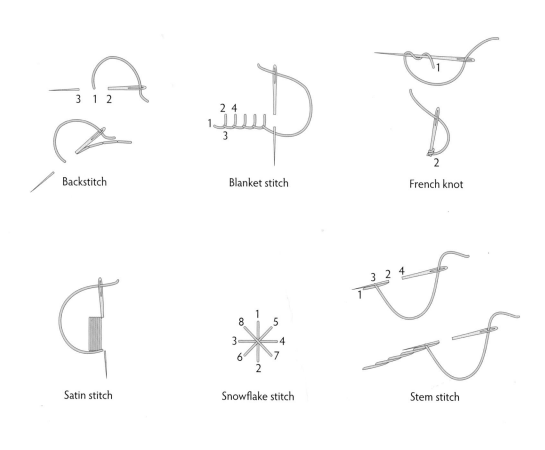

Backstitch

Blanket stitch

French knot

Satin stitch

Snowflake stitch

Stem stitch

Stipple stitches

# Snowman Stockings

These whimsical snowmen look a little worried about getting coal in their stockings, but Santa will be sure to smile when he sees them hanging from your mantel on Christmas Eve!

Designed and made by Mary Burns | Finished stockings: 8" x 19"

## Materials for 2 Stockings

*Yardage is based on 42"-wide fabric unless otherwise noted. Fat quarters measure 18" x 21".*

⅔ yard of blue wool for stockings

⅔ yard of Christmas print cotton for lining

¼ yard of cream wool for snowmen

6" x 9" piece of green wool for tree branches

5" x 9" piece of gold-plaid wool for scarves

Size 12 pearl cotton or 6-strand embroidery floss in brown and blue

Size 5 pearl cotton or 6-strand embroidery floss in red, gold, and white

8 blue buttons, ¾" diameter

Freezer paper

Fabric glue or stapler

Pencil or chalk marker

## Cutting

Patterns for stocking are on pages 71–74. Following the directions in the first sentence of "Piecing the Stocking" (page 68), join pattern pieces A–D to make a complete stocking pattern.

1. Trace the patterns for the stocking, the snowmen (pages 100–102), and the scarves (page 100) on the dull side of the freezer paper. Trace 13 tree branches. Cut out the shapes, leaving ¼" around the lines.

2. With a hot iron, press the freezer-paper templates to the blue wool as shown. Cut out four stocking pieces (two fronts and two backs). Also from the blue wool, cut two strips, 1" x 9", for hanging loops. Remove the stocking templates from the wool and iron onto the right side of the folded lining fabric. Cut out four stocking pieces (two facing left and two facing right) from the lining fabric.

3. With a hot iron, press the freezer-paper templates for the scarves to the gold-plaid wool, the templates for the snowmen bodies and heads to the cream wool, and the 13 branches to the green wool. Cut out the shapes.

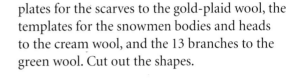

### Get the Most from Your Scraps

When cutting out the tree branches, iron 13 templates onto the wool at once to make sure they'll all fit on your piece of green wool. This saves time and wool! For identical templates like the snowman heads, cut just one template, press it to the appropriate fabric, cut out the shape, peel it off, reposition it, and then iron it on again.

## Embroidering the Stockings

1. Refer to the photo (page 96) when positioning the appliqués and marking lines for embroidery and to the embroidery-stitch diagrams (page 99) when embroidering. Instructions for embroidering the snowmen are the same for both stockings. To make sure the snowman body is in the right place on the stocking before you stitch it in place, lay out all of the appliqués on the blue-wool stocking before you begin stitching, and then remove all but the snowman body. Staple, glue, or pin the snowman body to the stocking front. Using a single strand of red pearl cotton, blanket-stitch the body in place, making stitches about ¼" long and ¼" apart.

2. Align the scarf along the top edge of the snowman body and staple, glue, or pin it in place; then blanket-stitch the edges using a single strand of black pearl cotton, stopping 1¼" from the left end and leaving the right end unattached. Cut five slits, 1" long, on the left end of the scarf for fringe.

3. Align the snowman head along the top edge of the scarf; staple, and then blanket-stitch in place with a single strand of red pearl cotton.

4. With a pencil or chalk marker, mark the location of the tree trunks as shown, measuring from the raw edge of the stocking. Using a double strand of brown pearl cotton, stem stitch the tree trunks.

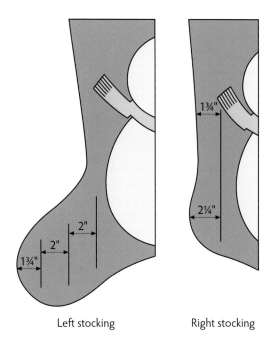

Left stocking        Right stocking

5. Position the tree branches on each trunk. Each branch shares roughly ¼" of the trunk with the branch above it. Blanket-stitch the branches in place with a single strand of brown pearl cotton, making stitches about ⅛" long and ⅛" apart.

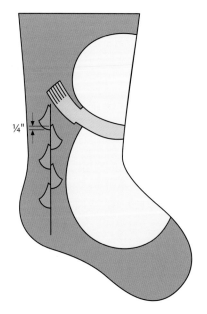

6. Measuring from the raw edges of the stocking, mark the location of the star. The vertical line of the star is 1¾" from the side raw edge and the top of the vertical line is 1¼" from the top raw edge of the stocking. The vertical line is 2½" long and the horizontal line is 1½" long. The diagonal lines are both 1" long. Using a double strand of gold pearl cotton, stem stitch the lines of the star. Refer to the photo (page 96) or the illustration below for snowflake placement. The snowflakes are each ½" in diameter. Using a double strand of white pearl cotton, make six ¼"-long straight stitches meeting in the center to create each snowflake.

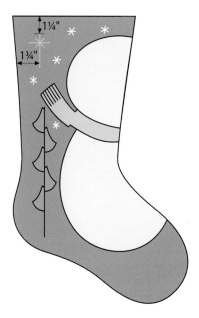

7. Using a pencil or chalk marker, mark the snowman smile and the location of the buttons. Using a double strand of black pearl cotton, stem stitch the smile. Use a double strand of blue pearl cotton to attach the buttons.

## Assembling the Stockings

1. Instructions for assembling the stockings are the same for both. With right sides together, align the stocking front and the lining front along the top edge. Stitch together along the top edge only using a ½" seam allowance. Press the seam allowances open to reduce bulk. Repeat to join the top edges of the stocking and lining backs.

2. Fold the 1" x 9" blue-wool strip in half and pin in position on the *right* side of the stocking, ½" from the just-sewn seam and on the same edge as the heel. Align the ends of the loop with the raw edges of the stocking. The rest of the loop will be out of sight in between the right sides of the front and back of the stocking. With right sides together and using a ½" seam allowance, sew the stocking/lining front unit to the stocking/lining back unit around all the outer edges. Leave a 4" opening for turning along the straightest part of the lining.

3. Clip the curves and turn the stocking right side out through the opening. Sew the opening closed by hand or machine. Tuck the lining inside the stocking. Press the edges smooth from the back of the stocking and topstitch ⅛" from the top of the stocking.

## Felting Your Own Wool

If you can't find felted wool at your local quilt shop, thrifting is an option. For these stockings, Mary felted her own wool from thrift-store finds. Look for high-quality 100% wool coats or wide skirts in good condition; the larger the size, the more wool you get for your money. Look for items with little or no interfacing (usually it's just around the buttons, waistbands, and collars). Start by cutting off all seams and interfaced parts to yield the largest pieces of wool you can. Machine wash with detergent on the hottest setting using high agitation. Machine dry on the hottest setting. Press with steam.

4"

½"

Loop

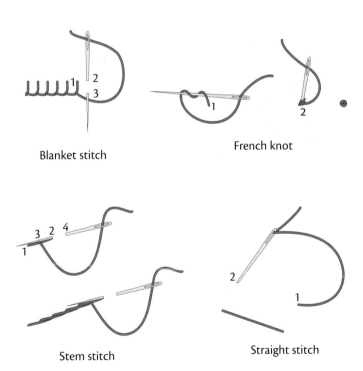

Blanket stitch

French knot

Stem stitch

Straight stitch

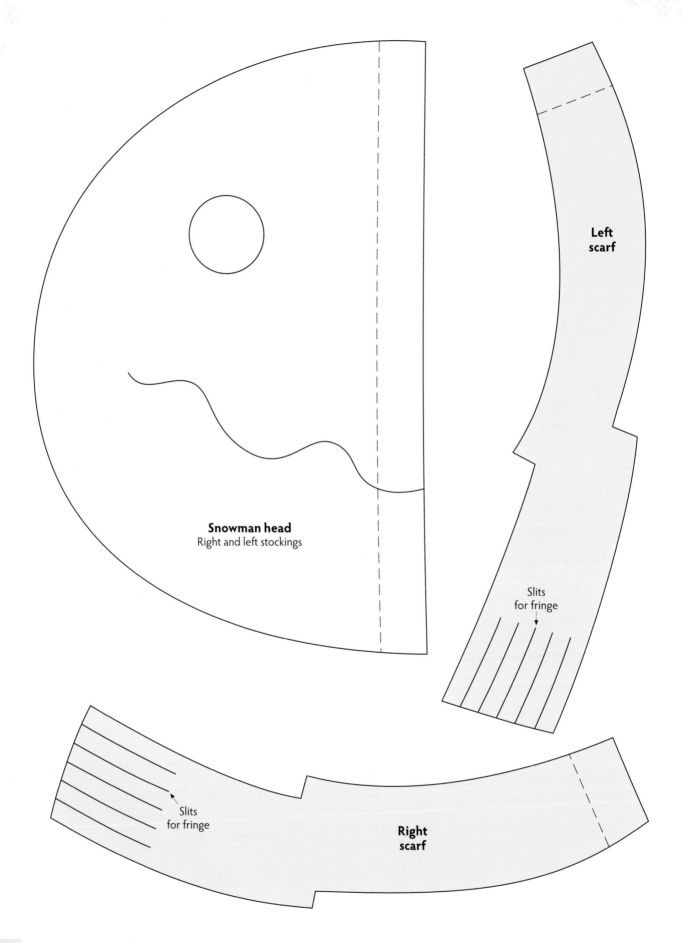

**Left scarf**

Slits
for fringe

**Snowman head**
Right and left stockings

Slits
for fringe

**Right scarf**

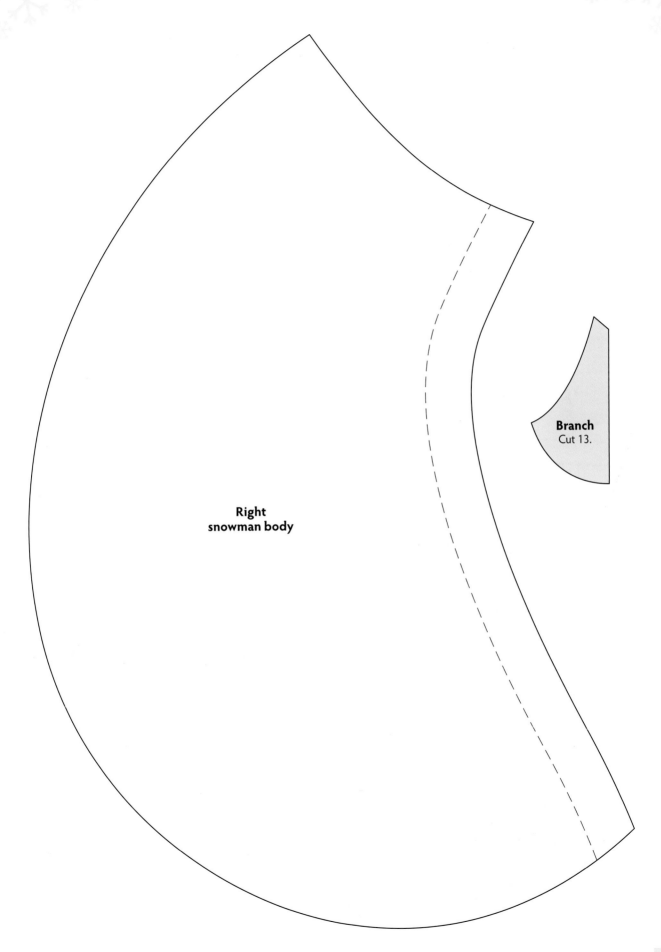

**Right
snowman body**

**Branch**
Cut 13.

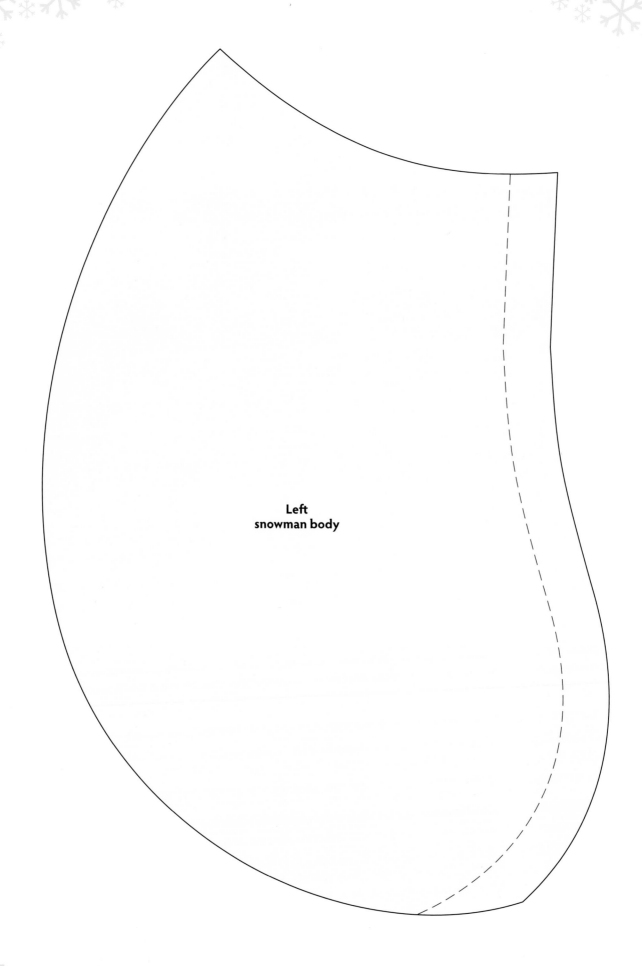

Left
snowman body

# Is it Time Yet?
# Advent Calendar

Cornelia grew up celebrating Christmas in the German tradition. As the years went on and her family became more "Americanized," they still kept up a favorite tradition—the Advent calendar. Naturally, she always wanted the ones that had a piece of chocolate behind the door! (What child wouldn't?!) And of course, it was *so* hard to wait.

Why not make your own Advent calendar that can be used year after year? You can tuck a different candy or trinket into the envelope for each day.

Designed and made by Cornelia Heitz Gauger  |  Finished quilt: 26½" x 32½"

## Materials

*Yardage is based on 42"-wide fabric.*

1 yard of red fabric for background

¾ yard of green polka dot for envelopes, fused lettering, and the number 25

24 assorted Christmas print 5" charm squares for envelopes

1 yard of fabric for backing

30" x 36" piece of thin batting or fusible fleece

1 roll of ¼"-wide fusible web

2 sheets, 8½" x 11", of paper-backed fusible web

1 sheet, 8½ x 11", of white printable fabric

Fabric glue

1 spool of elastic thread for loops

Pinking shears or pinking blade for your rotary cutter

Tweezers

Water-, air-, or heat-soluble marker

48 white buttons, ¼" diameter

2 wooden dowels, about 25" long

## Cutting

**From the red fabric, cut:**

1 rectangle, 30" x 36"

**From the green polka dot, cut:**

3 strips, 5" x 42"; crosscut into 24 squares, 5" x 5"

**From the backing fabric, cut:**

1 rectangle, 30" x 36"

4 squares, 5" x 5"

## Preparing the Background

1. Layer the 30" x 36" rectangles of backing, batting, and red fabric and baste. Lay the basted sandwich on a flat surface with the 36" sides running vertically. Beginning 4" from the bottom raw edge and 4" from the left side, use a ruler and water-, air-, or heat-soluble pen to draw a 5 x 5 grid of 4½" squares on the red fabric. At the top of the grid, draw a 6" x 22½" rectangle. These are your stitching lines.

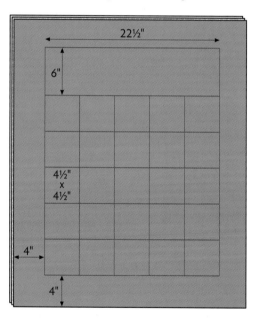

2. Using a decorative machine stitch, sew on the lines. A walking foot makes this easier. Cornelia used a continuous snowflake motif on her machine. Follow the manufacturer's instructions to erase the lines.

# Edging the Quilt and Adding Rod Pockets

1. Fold the red fabric to the front along one of the outside stitching lines and pin in place. Trim *only* the backing and batting 2" from the outer stitching line. Repeat on the other three sides. Check to be sure that the trimmed corners are square. The backing and batting *only* should now measure approximately 26½" x 32½". The top should measure approximately 30" x 36".

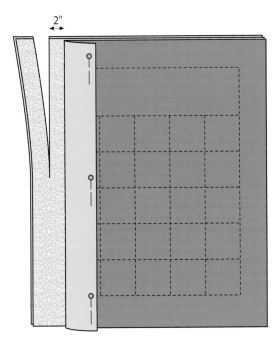

2. Trim the red 30" x 36" quilt top 1" *beyond* the trimmed backing and batting. The top *only* should now measure approximately 28" x 34".

3. Fold each corner of the front diagonally toward the back of the quilt and tuck it under the backing. Fold ½" of the front to the back on all sides and press. (The raw edges of the front will butt up against the raw edges of the backing.) Fold each of the four 5" backing fabric squares in half diagonally to make triangular rod-pocket corners. Press, and then baste in place on each corner of the trimmed backing. Fold the remaining ½" of the front over the edge of the backing, forming a mitered corner and covering the raw edges of both the backing and the rod pocket triangles; press. Pin or glue-baste in place, and then topstitch ⅜" from the edge of the quilt on all sides.

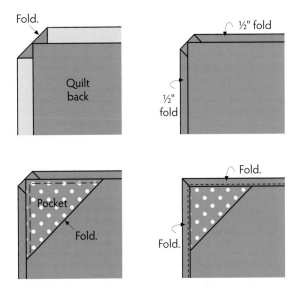

## Making the Envelopes

You will use one Christmas charm square and one green polka-dot square for each envelope.

1. On the wrong side of a polka-dot square, carefully place strips of ¼"-wide fusible web along each edge. Following the manufacturer's instructions, fuse the prepared square to the wrong side of one of the Christmas print squares, leaving one corner unfused. Trim all the way around the edges using pinking shears or your pinking blade.

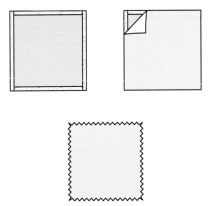

2. Fold a 1½" piece of elastic thread in half. Holding the ends together (tweezers come in really handy here!), place the ends on the unfused corner between the squares so that about ¼" of the loop extends diagonally beyond the corner. Tack the elastic in place with the tip of an iron, being careful not to touch the fusible web with the iron. Lay the unfused corner of the Christmas print square over the elastic thread and press the corner thoroughly with steam to make the bond permanent.

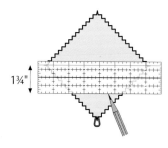

3. Put the fused square on your ironing surface, green polka-dot side up, with the elastic loop at the bottom. Fold the bottom corner up to meet the top corner and press well to form a crease at the center of the square. Unfold the square.

4. Place the 1¾" line of a ruler on the crease so the bottom edge of the ruler is 1¾" below the crease. Using a water-soluble pen or other disappearing marker, draw a line along the edge of the ruler.

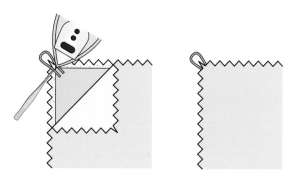

1¾"

Unfold.

5. Fold the square on the line, bringing the bottom point of the square to meet the center crease; press well and unfold.

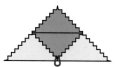

Fold and crease.

6. Fold the bottom edge of the square up along the center crease. Fold in both corners so their edges align with the fold and press well to complete the envelope. Make 24 total envelopes and set aside.

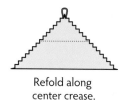

Refold along center crease.

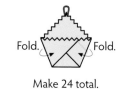

Fold.        Fold.

Make 24 total.

## Preparing the Letters and the 25

1. Trace the letters, question mark, and the numbers 2 and 5 (pages 108 and 109) onto the paper side of the fusible web. Patterns are reversed to use with fusible web. Cut out the shapes, leaving ¼" around the traced lines. Following the manufacturer's instructions, press the fusible web to the wrong side of the green polka-dot fabric. Cut out the appliqués on the traced line. Referring to the quilt photo (page 103), lay out the letters at the top of the quilt to spell out *Is it Time Yet?* in a way that looks pleasing to you. Fuse the letters in place.

2. Center the number *25* in the bottom right-hand square and fuse in place.

## Preparing the Envelope Numbers

Photocopy the small numbers (page 108) onto an 8½" x 11" sheet of printable fabric, and then back the fabric with an 8½" x 11" piece of fusible web. Cut each circle out carefully.

## Attaching the Envelopes

1. Play with the placement of the envelopes to determine which envelope you want in which square. When you find the placement that you like, fuse the corresponding number (upright) onto the flap of each envelope, just below the elastic loop.

2. Put a thin layer of fabric glue on the *back* of envelope 1.

3. Center the first envelope in the top-left square and lay it in place. Press with a dry iron to help the glue dry faster. Repeat for each of the remaining 23 envelopes.

4. When the glue is dry, use a tacking stitch to secure the side points together.

5. Sew a ¼" button just above the top point of the open flap and just below the bottom of the envelope.

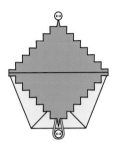

6. Fill with candy or trinkets and let the count-down begin!

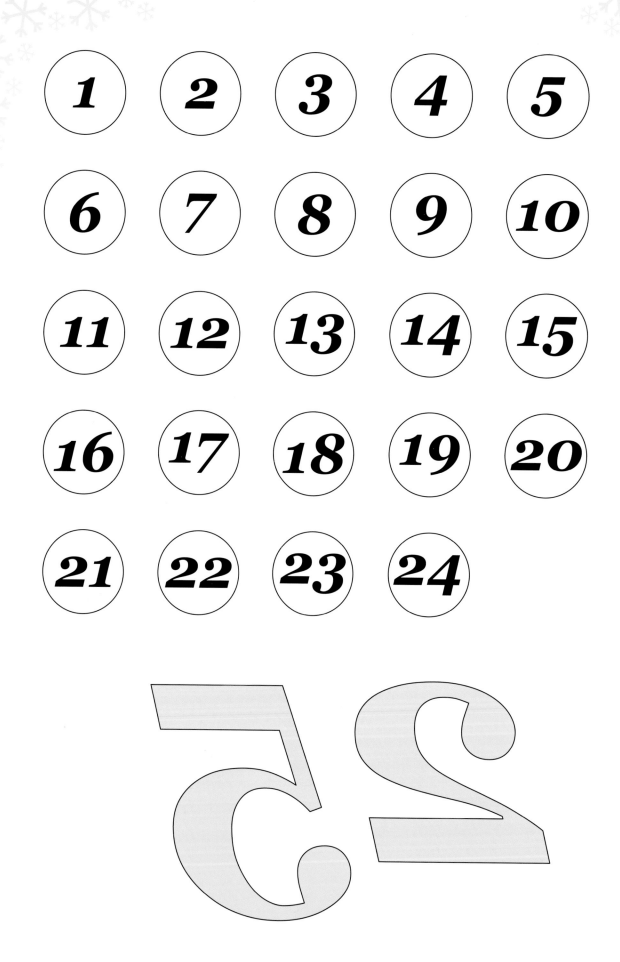

Is it

Time

Yet?

# O Tannenbaum Pillow

L uxurious hand-dyed wools add elegance to this folksy design. Enjoy this fun project while stitching by the fire as Christmas draws near. How lovely are these branches!

Designed and made by Mary Burns  |  Finished pillow: 14" x 28"

## Materials

*Yardage is based on 42"-wide fabric.*

16" x 30" piece of white or cream wool for pillow front

10" x 15" piece of green felted wool for branches

½ yard of Christmas print cotton fabric for pillow back

Size 12 brown pearl cotton

Size 5 gold pearl cotton

14" x 28" pillow form

Freezer paper

Pencil or chalk marker

Fabric glue or stapler

## Cutting

**From the white or cream wool, cut:**

1 rectangle, 15" x 29"

**From the backing fabric, cut:**

2 pieces, 15" x 18¾"

## Cutting Out the Branches

1. Trace the branch pattern (page 112) five times on the dull side of the freezer paper. Cut out the branches. Iron the shiny side of the freezer-paper templates to the green wool, keeping them close together so as to not waste wool.

2. Cut out the five branches. Reuse the templates to cut a total of 25 branches.

## Embroidering the Trees and Star

Refer to the embroidery stitch diagrams (page 99), if needed.

1. Referring to the illustration below for placement, mark lines (in the lengths indicated) on the white wool 15" x 29" rectangle using a light pencil or chalk marker. Using the pattern (page 112), draw the star an equal distance from both the third and fourth tree trunks as shown.

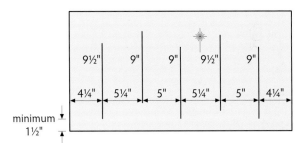

2. Using *two* strands of brown pearl cotton, stem-stitch along the marked lines to make the tree trunks. Referring to the photo (page 110), position the tree branches on either side of each trunk. Notice that each branch shares ½" of its trunk with the branch above it. Glue or staple the branches in place. Blanket-stitch the branches to the background with *one* strand of brown pearl cotton, making stitches about ⅛" long and ⅛" apart. You may wish to take an extra tacking stitch at the points of the branches to hold the floss in place.

3. Using *one* strand of gold pearl cotton, stem-stitch the vertical and horizontal lines of the star. Add French knots and straight stitches as indicated.

## Assembling the Pillow

1. Turn under and press a ¾"-wide hem on one 15" edge of each backing piece. Turn under an additional 1" and press. Topstitch ⅛" from the fold and again ⅛" from the edge of hem.

2. Layer the appliquéd top and backing pieces right sides together, aligning the raw edges and overlapping the hemmed edges of the backing pieces by about 5" at the center.

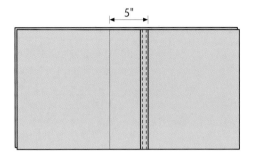

3. Pin in place. Using a ½" seam allowance, stitch all the way around the pillow cover. Trim diagonally across the corners and turn the pillow cover right side out. Press, rolling the seam allowances with your fingers to flatten them.

4. Insert the pillow form and enjoy!

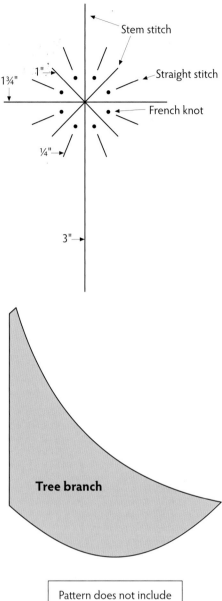

**Tree branch**

Pattern does not include seam allowance.

## What's your creative passion?
### Find it at ShopMartingale.com
books • eBooks • ePatterns • daily blog • free projects
videos • tutorials • inspiration • giveaways

**Martingale**
*Create with Confidence*